Songs of Freedom

Stories of lives transformed by the deep power of Christ

Edited by **Eileen Mitson**
with Commentary by **Steve Goss**

MONARCH
B O O K S
Oxford, UK, and Grand Rapids, Michigan, USA

First published in the UK in 2005 by Monarch Books
(a publishing imprint of Lion Hudson plc),
Mayfield House, 256 Banbury Road, Oxford OX2 7DH
Tel: +44 (0) 1865 302750   Fax: +44 (0) 1865 302757

ISBN-13: 978-1-85424-719-3 (UK)
ISBN-10: 1-85424-719-0 (UK)
ISBN-13: 978-0-8254-6099-0 (USA)
ISBN-10: 0-8254-6099-9 (USA)

Distributed by:
UK: Marston Book Services Ltd, PO Box 269,
Abingdon, Oxon OX14 4YN
USA: Kregel Publications, PO Box 2607,
Grand Rapids, Michigan 49501
Worldwide co-edition produced by Lion Hudson plc,
Mayfield House, 256 Banbury Road, Oxford OX2 7DH
Tel: +44 (0) 1865 302750   Fax: +44 (0) 1865 302757
Email: coed@lionhudson.com <mail to: co-ed@lionhudson.com>
www.lionhudson.com <http://www.lionhudson-publishing.com>

British Library Cataloguing Data
A catalogue record for this book is available
from the British Library.

Printed in Great Britain.

Contents

Note:
some of the names have been changed
to avoid identification

Foreword

by Neil Anderson

God created Adam and Eve to be physically and spiritually alive. Had they lived the way God intended, they could have lived for ever. They chose, however, to decide for themselves what was right and wrong, and their sin separated them from God. They died spiritually, and their souls were separated from God. Physical death was to be a consequence as well, and their souls separated from their bodies, which returned to dust.

As a result of Adam and Eve's disobedience, all their descendants would be born physically alive but spiritually dead. The fall affected all humanity, and there was no way they could save themselves. Going to church, practising spiritual disciplines and trying to live righteous lives could not restore what Adam and Eve had lost, which was spiritual (eternal) life. No matter how hard we try, our sin will separate us from God.

But there is good news. God sent His own Son to pay the penalty for our sins. By shedding His own blood on the cross, Jesus removed the enmity that exists between God and us. But the Gospel is much more. Jesus came to give us life – spiritual life. Those who put their trust in God are born again spiritually. Their souls are in union with God. The resurrection of Jesus Christ from the dead ensures that every true believer has eternal life in Christ.

Eternal life is not something believers get when they physically die. They receive eternal/spiritual life the moment they are born again. The apostle John wrote, "He who has the Son has life; he who does not have the Son of God does not have life" (1 John 5:12). By faith alone we are alive and free in Christ. Our sins are forgiven and "there

5

is now no condemnation for those who are in Christ Jesus" (Romans 8:1). Every born-again believer is alive and free in Christ, but how many are living that way?

If all the above is true, then why aren't more Christians living liberated lives in Christ? And why do we still struggle with many of the same old problems, and often feel as we did before we experienced salvation? Because we were all born dead (spiritually) in our trespasses and sins (Ephesians 2:1, Authorised Version). We had neither the presence of God in our lives nor the knowledge of His ways. So we all learned to live our lives independently of God. Then one day we came to Christ, and were transported out of the kingdom of darkness into the kingdom of God (Colossians 1:13). We became new creations in Christ, and old things passed away (2 Corinthians 5:17). But nobody pushed the clear or delete button in our minds. In fact, there isn't a delete button. That is why Paul wrote, "Do not conform any longer to the pattern of this world, but be transformed by the renewing of your mind. Then you will be able to test and approve what God's will is – his good, pleasing and perfect will" (Romans 12:2). The idea is, "no longer be conformed to this world", because we all were, and we still can be. As believers we can read the wrong literature, see the wrong movies and have the wrong friends.

We renew our minds by studying God's word and by having fellowship with other believers. We learn to walk by faith according to what God says is true in the power of the Holy Spirit. It sounds rather simple, but there are barriers to our growth in Christ. The world, the flesh and the devil will seek to lure us away from God and impede our growth in Christ. Therefore, we are instructed to not love the world, to overcome the flesh and to resist the devil. Those who don't overcome the opposition, or don't know how to, find themselves in conflict, and their growth is stunted. Addressing those who have failed to grow, Paul wrote:

> **Brothers, I could not address you as spiritual but as worldly – mere infants in Christ. I gave you milk, not solid food, for you**

**were not yet ready for it. Indeed, you are still not ready. You
are still worldly. For since there is jealousy and quarrelling
among you, are you not worldly? Are you not acting like mere
men? (1 Corinthians 3:1–3)**

There must be some way to resolve jealousy and strife if people are
going to be able to grow spiritually and bear fruit, and there is. There
are many opportunities to grow in our faith, but few opportunities to
repent, which we are instructed to do. I have spent most of my adult
life learning how to help people resolve their personal and spiritual
conflicts through genuine repentance, and faith in God. I made little
progress until I realised that I was not the "Wonderful Counsellor".
Only Jesus could set the captive free and bind up the broken-hearted.
True Christian counselling is an encounter with God, which I explain in
my book *Discipleship Counselling* (Regal Books, 2003).

In this book you will read powerful testimonies from God's children who have overcome bitterness, fear, depression, anxiety, abuse
and the occult. Truth sets us free, but, if we want to experience that
freedom, we have to repent. For the repentance to be complete we
must submit to God and resist the devil, who will flee from us (James
4:7). The tool we use to help others is called *The Steps to Freedom in
Christ* (Steps). It is important to know that The Steps don't set you
free. The one who sets you free is Christ, and what sets you free is
your response to Him in repentance and faith. This is something you
can accomplish on your own. It would be considerably easier to do if
you read *Victory over the Darkness* and *The Bondage Breaker* first. The
Steps are included in *The Bondage Breaker*, or they can be purchased
separately through the office of Freedom in Christ Ministries or your
local Christian bookshop.

The testimonies in this book will mention the above material, but,
as the author, I want you to know that I am sharing with you *a way*,
but Jesus is *The Way*. I want to give you *an answer* for your problems,
but Jesus is *The Answer*. I want to offer you some hope, but *Jesus Is
Our Hope*. He loves you in spite of what you have done, or what has

been done to you, and He will set you free and bind up your broken heart if you will let Him. I can't fix your past and neither does Jesus, but He will set you free from it. Being alive and free in Christ is the birthright of every child of God, and you can experience that yourself if you will put your trust in Him and be willing to resolve your personal and spiritual conflicts through genuine repentance. May the good Lord enable you to do just that.

Dr Neil T. Anderson
Founder and President Emeritus of Freedom in Christ Ministries

Introduction

I count it a privilege to have been given the responsibility of putting together these personal stories from people whose lives have been changed by applying the biblical approach taught by Freedom in Christ Ministries. This advocates a structured process of repentance called "The Steps to Freedom in Christ", and helps us understand the amazing truths of what Jesus has already done for every Christian. The Steps encourage us to claim our own freedom by repenting and choosing to believe the truth.

Each of the contributors to this book has a unique and often deeply moving story to tell, and I would like to thank them for co-operating with us in being willing to share the secrets of their hearts in this way. For most of them, this will have been a costly thing to do. But their hope is that others who have found themselves in similar circumstances will be helped and comforted by what they read here.

There is a common denominator to each of these testimonies, for each person has travelled on a journey of mental pain and emotional bondage to a new freedom – a freedom that, for some, had once seemed an unattainable dream. One of them has described her own experience as "stepping out into the Promised Land". Some speak of having been brought "out of darkness into God's marvellous light". Others describe how they finally came to the place where they felt a great weight had been lifted from their shoulders. And all of them are finding different ways of sharing their new-found joy with others. At the same time, they are learning the importance of discipleship and of putting on "the whole armour of God".

Several of the writers emphasise that simply following the Freedom in Christ teaching and submitting oneself to the "Steps to

Freedom" is by no means a quick fix. But in most cases it has proved to be the breakthrough that they so desperately needed. They then went on to learn about discipleship, and to walk in the freedom they had claimed.

There are a variety of stories. Not all are from people with obviously troubled backgrounds. Some are simply "ordinary" Christians who, all the same, have had hidden needs that have crippled their spiritual life and robbed them of their God-given right to peace and joy.

As we read their stories, we are reminded once more that among those who sit regularly in our churches are folk who are hiding aching hearts and troubled minds behind a façade of cheerfulness. Some may not even bother to put on the façade, but sit there week after week in the hope that some word will be spoken that will give an answer to the torturing questions that nag away at the back of their minds. In most of the stories the healing process took place in the context of a loving local church where ordinary people were prepared to spend time encouraging others to take hold of the truth.

The world is full of people with hidden needs. But where are those who are ready and able to meet those needs? Where is the sensitivity and compassion that is able to reach beyond the outward expression to the inner pain? Many of the people who have shared their stories say that it was the love and concern of individuals who came alongside them that was so precious and meaningful. And churches who are using the Freedom in Christ approach are finding that they are able to see even those with more deeply rooted problems take hold of their freedom and go on to become fruitful disciples.

Alongside the suffering of these souls in torment (for that is how many of them would describe their lives prior to discovering their path to freedom) is the suffering of the families and loved ones who have to stand helplessly by and watch, unable to do anything to relieve either their own pain or that of the ones in their care. This is especially true of those who care for victims of mental illness. But it also applies to any situation where lives are spinning out of control.

Some parents have shared with us the way in which God sustained them through horrific experiences of this kind. Others, who lost one child to cancer and then had to watch another live through years of psychotic illness, have said that the mental illness was even harder to bear than the death of their child. For during these times the patient is incapable of giving or receiving love, but exists in a state of darkness and distortion.

P. D. James, the well-known crime writer, whose husband suffered from mental illness, writes this: "Only those who have lived with the mental illness of someone they love can understand what this entails. One suffers with the patient and for oneself. Another human being, who was once a beloved companion, can become not only a stranger, but occasionally a malevolent stranger."

One thing is certain: whatever the true underlying causes of mental illness are, the evil one can often gain a foothold through negative emotions. This means that a child who has been hurt emotionally, by whatever cause, often goes on to harbour angry and resentful thoughts towards those whom he imagines to be the cause of his pain. There may be jealousy, too, where other siblings are concerned, or guilt about misdemeanours that come back to haunt him in weak moments. These dark thoughts quickly begin to fester and Satan moves in with his systematic programme of lies. He may take on any one of his familiar guises – an angel of light (2 Corinthians 11:14); a roaring lion (1 Peter 5:8); or simply a nagging voice that taunts and tortures the troubled mind. Ultimately, his trump card is to convince the sufferer that he is worthless. Images of death and destruction then further deepen the patient's despair. Self-harm and suicidal impulses seem to offer the only release, for this enemy is without mercy.

The child of God struggles against such attacks in vain until he learns to submit to God and resist the devil, at which point the enemy has no choice but to flee (see James 4:7). When light eventually breaks through, there is "joy unspeakable".

The writers of these stories want to share that joy with you so that you too may know that true freedom is the birthright of every

Christian, no matter what has happened in their life or how dire their present circumstances may seem.

At the end of the book there is some encouragement for you if you too want to walk in a greater measure of the freedom that Christ has won for you.

Eileen Mitson

Chapter 1

Does the Gospel really work?

"What a strange question to ask. Of course the Gospel works!"

That's the answer I would have given a few years ago. I had a reasonable grasp of theology, I was in a leadership position in a church and I had a bit of a preaching ministry. Yet, if I'm honest, although I really did believe that the Good News that Jesus came to bring worked at one level, at another level I had no answers.

In my own life, I found myself caught in cycles of sin that I just didn't seem to get out of. I think I had concluded that I'd just have to grin and bear it and do my best until Jesus came back and took me to heaven. I'd certainly given up any hope of escaping from those problems.

As one of the leaders of a local church, I was at even more of a loss. People sometimes came to me with concerns they were struggling with and I didn't have a clue how to help them. I would pray with them and talk with them, but nothing much seemed to change. In the end, it was easier to avoid them!

As I look back, I guess I knew all along that Jesus was the answer. I just didn't know *how*. Yet all along the solution had been staring me in the face. Jesus said plainly, "You will know the truth, and the truth will set you free" (John 8:32). Of course, I thought I already knew the truth, and on one level I did. But I now realise that just having facts in my head was very different from really knowing the truth. The breakthrough came when I "connected" with the truth in a real way.

I am privileged to visit many churches in the course of my work for Freedom in Christ Ministries. As I do so, I meet many Christians who have given up any hope that they can move on. They seem to be waiting for God or someone else to "zap" them – and most have been waiting a long time. I also meet hard-working, compassionate leaders who are at a loss as to how to help those who come to them with troubling issues. They've tried praying for them. They've tried visiting them. They've tried everything they can think of. But not much seems to change.

The true stories that follow are written by ordinary Christians, most of whom felt at one time that there was no way forward, no hope for change. Yet, with the help of other ordinary Christians in ordinary churches, they discovered the extraordinary truth that in Christ they already had everything they needed; they had life in all its fullness.

As you read these stories, I know you will be encouraged and that your faith and hope in God will be renewed – the God who delights to bring hope where there was none, who loves to turn those who feel the most broken into fruitful disciples. You will also understand the process by which every Christian can make those deep connections with Jesus, who is the truth.

When I first met Rachel, she was the epitome of a Christian who had lost all hope. She was covered in bandages from injuries that she had inflicted on herself. She had difficulty stringing two sentences together because of drug abuse. She had suffered from eating disorders for years. In fact, it's a miracle she was alive at all.

We've put her story first because it's a powerful demonstration that Jesus offers a way out, even for those who find themselves in the most difficult and apparently hopeless circumstances.

We'll hear firstly from her parents, David and Mary, and then from Rachel herself.

David and Mary's story

"I love you both, and I'm sorry it had to end like this..."

It was November 1994 when our 17-year-old daughter handed me a note she had written. "Mum, I want you to read this – it will tell you what's wrong with me. I've been to the doctor and I've seen a friend. Don't be cross, will you?" she said anxiously. I took the note and nervously opened it. My worst fears were confirmed. Rachel was suffering from bulimia. I had already guessed but now it was out in the open. A feeling of relief came over me, mixed with feelings of despair. Why? How? What next?

Some months earlier, I had been talking to a friend and had shared with her that I was worried Rachel was heading for a serious eating disorder. Since that time Rachel had gradually given up eating breakfast and also stopped taking her packed lunch to college.

Then one day she said, "Mum, don't cook me dinner tonight, I'll do my own."

"OK, but why aren't you eating breakfast and lunch?" I asked. "Because I want to have a big eat-up in the evening," she replied.

I knew that she was buying large quantities of chocolate from the shop next door to our house. This was when I began to wonder if she was bingeing and maybe suffering from bulimia.

David and I were naturally very worried about her. Our GP put her on an antidepressant and explained that there was an underlying reason for her bulimia. He said he could help her with her eating once she had sorted out the problem. Not knowing how to deal with the situation, I started buying extra food for her to binge on. I panicked a month later, when our family food bill doubled! So I sought advice from our GP, who told me I should not be buying Rachel's binge food: it was her responsibility.

As time went on the bingeing increased, until it was happening five or six times a day. At first it was always done in secret, but eventually Rachel would take over our kitchen and dining room. Several times I heard her demanding that Sue, her younger sister, leave the room because she needed to binge. Bingeing took place at night too. It was most unpleasant waking up in the middle of the night to the smell of cooking. We were often finding food missing from the fridge, freezer and cupboards. When she was desperate enough, Rachel would even eat from the rubbish bin.

Soon she stopped eating with the family and just binged all day. She kept her food in a plastic storage box that became known as the "binge box". On several occasions when I came down in the morning I would find the binge box in the kitchen – a sign that she had been up in the night. In sheer frustration I would empty the contents all over the kitchen floor. I felt angry, frustrated and helpless. Nothing David and I said to her was of any use. How was she ever going to stop this way of living? What could we do? And what was the cause of it all?

As the months passed Rachel finished her college course, and in June 1996 started her nursing training. By this time she was losing weight rapidly and often complained about how fat she was. We had begun to see the signs of anorexia. She had lost most of her friends and now found socialising very difficult. Her relationships with me, her father and her sister and brother were growing steadily worse. Even her boyfriend didn't know how to cope with her.

Rachel moved into the nurses' home at the local hospital. We didn't feel she was well enough but, as she was determined to do this and it would give us a much-needed break, we gave her our full support. Making friends was almost impossible and a lot of time was spent in bingeing, drinking and self-harming. Rachel would steal from the other students when her binge food ran out. The one friendship she did make was with another student who also suffered from bulimia and had a problem with alcohol and self-harm. They found they could relate well to one another but we felt they just encouraged each other in bad ways. Her work deteriorated and she would often let staff down when she was supposed to be doing a shift at the hospital. She was too weak most days to get up and would spend long periods of time asleep on her bed.

At the end of the first term, Rachel came home to see us. It was the August bank holiday. What a shock it was to see her! She was so thin that she could hardly walk and she looked dreadful. She sat on the sofa with a blanket around her and a hot water bottle because she was so cold. We were having a heat wave at the time! She could not reach out for a cup of tea because she was so weak. I asked her when she had last eaten – she didn't know. We suggested that she move back home and we would try to help her start eating again in order to build herself up.

We went to see her course tutor, who advised Rachel to take a term off and to get better before recommencing her studies. Instead of getting better she grew steadily worse, and had to give up her nursing training altogether.

The days and nights became difficult for Rachel. Her sleeping pattern changed until she slept all day and was awake all night. She was relying heavily on drugs and drink to help her sleep. Often Rachel would spend the night clubbing in the town and we would lie awake wondering where she was and whom she was with. We never knew what time she would come home. We just prayed that God would protect her and keep her safe. She would arrive home about two or three in the morning, having walked from town. We would go downstairs and find her slumped in the hall because she had drunk too much, and would try to get her up the stairs to bed –

thankful that she was at last safely home. It was some time later that we discovered that she had been raped and assaulted on more than one occasion; she was in such a state that she would stand outside clubs when drunks were leaving, not caring what happened to her.

Another way of spending her nights was to creep downstairs when everyone was asleep and watch horror videos. We were horrified when we found out that she was filling her mind with such evil. She has since told us that she would watch them over and over again, often trying to find videos that were worse than the previous ones.

In April 1997 she was admitted to an eating disorders unit, where she was made to eat three meals a day. Everything on the plate had to be eaten even if it got cold. The bathrooms were locked for an hour after every meal and the patients had to sit quietly during that time. It was while she was there that she was given sleeping pills to help her through the night. After only two weeks she was discharged and continued as an outpatient on a daily basis for a further ten weeks. We discovered later that during her time as an outpatient she had been deceiving us all. She was telling us that she would have her breakfast and evening meal at the eating disorders unit and telling them that she would be eating those meals at home. This meant that she was able to eat only lunch and to starve herself for the rest of the time. Rachel was eventually discharged after twelve weeks, but although she was eating much better when she came out it wasn't long before she slipped back into her old patterns.

There came a time when she did seem a little better. We got the impression that she was seeking help and, having written for some time to a Christian lady who had herself recovered from anorexia some years before, Rachel arranged to spend four days with her. During her stay there she received prayer and counselling and actually reached the point where she wanted to renounce the bulimia. When she returned home she threw out her cigarettes and alcohol and burned all her drawings and paintings connected with the horror videos she had been watching. There was some improvement during the next few months but gradually the addictions crept back. She had been warned that if she did not sincerely desire to give up her illness then her other addictions would return.

Rachel managed to do some voluntary work at the local hospital and over the next few months she gradually increased her hours until she was working full-time. She was very keen to go back to her nursing training even though people around her were advising her not to go back too soon. Rachel applied and was accepted – starting work in September 1998. However, during this time her addictions continued to be a problem and visits to A & E were frequent. She had also begun to shoplift to aid her bulimia, and this led to the stealing of prescriptions from her GP in order to get hold of more sleeping tablets. She was now having regular nightmares and her screaming would wake everybody up. Some years earlier we had discovered that a workman had sexually abused Rachel in our own home when she was twelve years old. She had kept this secret for six years. The events surrounding this horrific attack were coming back to her in her nightmare, along with an evil-looking character called Freddy from one of her horror videos. We could see the fear in her face as we went to help her, and it was often very difficult to console her and to assure her that these things were not really happening. This would happen several times a night and Rachel began to be afraid to go to sleep.

She managed to complete a year of her nursing training but was extremely unwell and eventually had to give up. The bulimia, anorexia, self-harm, overdosing on sleeping tablets and laxatives and alcohol took its toll on her small, weak body. She was nearly always sleepy and confused and the tensions at home were enormous. Whenever she was admitted to hospital for a few days we found a measure of relief. But we knew she would be back with more "drama" for us all to contend with.

Life became a nightmare for us all. We just clung to our faith, and to the belief that God would see us through and that He would somehow bring healing to Rachel, but our faith was sorely tried at times. Over the months that followed we had several visits from the police to search Rachel's room for stolen items such as prescriptions and tablets. Most of her clothes were ones she had stolen; she was heavily in debt and she admitted to us that she had "lost her conscience". It was all really heartbreaking.

Just when we thought things couldn't get any worse we received a phone call while on holiday in Yorkshire. Rachel had been involved in a car accident while away at camp, and although not injured she was very unwell. The leaders of the camp felt that she needed to be at home. Our other daughter, Sue, insisted that we must not cut short our holiday – she would collect Rachel and take her home. So Sue made a three-hundred-mile round trip to get her sister safely back home. It was later on that week that the story surrounding the accident unfolded. Rachel and a male friend had actually stolen his father's car to go shopping. Rachel was driving while under the influence of alcohol and had pulled out in front of another car. The police said that if they had not been travelling in a people carrier they would almost certainly both have been killed. Once again we thanked God for His hand of protection. This eventually came to court. Rachel had previously been let off several shoplifting incidents with a warning and now we thought she would be in real trouble. However, owing to her deteriorating health, she was given a two-year suspended sentence. If she did anything wrong during this time they would bring up all the offences listed against her in court. It was a stern warning.

One day in November 1999 while Rachel was out I took something up to her room, and there on her bed was a note written to her dad and me. It said, "I never committed suicide because I thought it was selfish to you – to do that to you. But now especially since what Mum said I realise that it is selfish for me to stay alive, so thank you for the life I did enjoy. I love you both and am sorry it had to end like this. Love Rach X." I snatched up the note and rushed downstairs to show it to David. Where was she? Had she really gone somewhere to die? Would she be back? What should we do? What did I say that made her write this note?

We phoned the police, her GP, her psychiatrist and any-one else who might know anything. About half an hour later she walked through the front door. I was beside myself with worry and in floods of tears.

"Mum, whatever is the matter?" she said, her face full of concern.

"I found this note on your bed," I sobbed.

"Oh no," she said. "You weren't meant to see that yet!"

"What do you mean, 'yet'?" I said.

She then explained that she had planned to end it all. She had been out to buy food for a last binge; after that she had been going to slit her wrists, overdose and deliberately crash her car to make sure it really happened this time. The note was ready to put into an envelope and be addressed to us both. This was planned for later in the day.

"Mum, I didn't know that this is how you would react," she said. "I thought you would be relieved if I went!"

We assured her that this was the last thing we wanted. "We would never get over it! We want you better!"

"Well," she said, "I won't do it now that I know what it would do to you..."

We phoned all the people we had contacted to let them know she was safe at home. I thanked the Lord for letting me find that note. Rachel spent the next five or six weeks on a psychiatric ward at the local hospital.

It was a Sunday morning at the end of May 2000 when I awoke to find that David had taken Rachel to A & E in the early hours. She had argued with him about something and had then gone upstairs, locked her door and cut herself. Then she had come down and said, "Now look what you've made me do!"

"Right," he said, "I'm taking you to A & E," whereupon she rushed upstairs again and took a potentially lethal quantity of antidepressants. David walked in just as she was taking the last mouthful, and, not knowing exactly what she had taken, insisted that she went to A & E.

Rachel had spent the previous two weekends in hospital following overdoses on antidepressants. It was becoming almost a "normal" event in the life of our family. During the afternoon the phone rang. It was a lady doctor from the intensive care unit at the hospital. She sounded very solemn. She explained that Rachel had had a fit due to the overdose and was on a ventilator to give her body a rest. It was at this moment that David realised he had saved her life by taking her to A & E in the night. We went to see her not knowing how we would find her; there were tubes coming in and out of her body all over the place. She didn't know we were there.

I remember feeling very numb but also feeling oddly comforted by all the tubes because I knew they were supporting her tiny, frail body. I sat and watched the feeding tube as it pumped nourishment into her. When we saw her the next day she was awake, wondering why she was there and certainly not happy to have a feeding tube. The staff left her connected to one of the monitors so that it would be harder for her to just get up and leave. She had discharged herself on many occasions. Her psychiatrist visited her after two days and said that he didn't think she needed to be admitted to the psychiatric ward. We could not believe this – nor could the hospital staff! Surely she needed urgent support and treatment. But after three days she was discharged and we took her home.

Throughout the first half of 2001 Rachel was admitted to A & E every weekend and often during the week as well, for various reasons. She was taking four different types of sleeping tablet as well as other non-prescription sleeping aids, and would often take a whole week's supply in one go. Other overdoses included painkillers, and these nearly always resulted in her being treated with a special drip for several hours. A frightening day for her sister was when Rachel was so drugged on sleeping tablets that she microwaved the electric kettle!

We were becoming more and more tired to the point of exhaustion with what was happening and it felt as if nobody could do anything for Rachel except patch her up and send her home. At the beginning of December Rachel was in A & E again. We had called four ambulances in twelve days, the overdosing was causing her to have fits, and her arms were constantly bandaged from all the self-harm by means of cutting and scalding. We were so exhausted and emotionally drained and just felt we could not go on like this any more; the situation was affecting every part of our lives including our everyday work. We made the decision to tell the doctors that we could not have Rachel back home. It was a hard decision and one that we did not make lightly. We knew Rachel would take it badly and think that we didn't love her any more, but we also felt that it was time to force something to be done for her.

Rachel spent three days in A & E and was then moved to the psychiatric ward; there she remained for nearly nine months and during that time her psychiatrist told her there was one more option left for her – to be admitted to a Crisis Recovery Unit in a hospital in South London. The CRU refused to take her at first because they felt at the time that her self-harming was at a dangerous level and it would be difficult for her to work in an environment in which she would have to take responsibility for her own safety. So it was about fifteen months later in fact that Rachel went into the CRU. There were twelve people on this unit and each had their own room. During the week there were a number of group and individual therapy sessions. Weekends were to be spent at home with the family. We were worried about this arrangement because we knew that while at home she would do anything she could to harm herself.

A month later her sister, Sue, was married and Rachel was bridesmaid. She was very excited about this and we did everything we could to help her get through the day. We had encouraged her not to cut her arms so that she didn't have to wear bandages. She made a real effort and her arms began to heal. Instead she cut her legs – something that she now regrets! Rachel seemed to cope very well that day and many family and friends remarked on how well she looked. However, as soon as we arrived home, she deliberately scalded her arm. She said she didn't fit in at CRU but we felt it was a reaction to the wedding day. Rachel had often talked about how jealous she was of her younger sister. Sue had lots of friends, had done well at school, been to university and gained a degree, drove her own car and was now married and about to go off on honeymoon. In Rachel's eyes Sue had everything.

We tried to find out how her treatment at CRU was going, but the staff wouldn't tell us because of patient confidentiality, and Rachel herself didn't want to talk about it. We did notice, however, that Rachel seemed to be deteriorating in many ways. She began to watch horror movies again while on the unit and said she could feel an evil presence in her room. She constantly overdosed, self-harmed, smoked heavily and drank alcohol.

The turning point for Rachel came in an unexpected way and one that was totally out of our hands. One particular weekend, Rachel told us she wasn't coming home but was going to stay with a patient friend and her family. This worried us, but as she was now 25 we decided she was free to do what she wanted. I prayed that, if anything happened to her, God would use it for her good. That prayer was answered... she overdosed on something before leaving the CRU on the Friday because she felt she could not cope with people she did not know. By the time she reached her friend's house she was in such a bad way that she ended up in hospital for the night. On returning to the CRU on Monday morning she was told that, because she had not reported what she had done, she was now on enforced leave for a week so that she could think about her irresponsible behaviour. This all seemed very strange to us, because she was going to miss a week's treatment. And we were going to have to have her at home for a week when we could barely cope with her for a weekend.

We had to tell her we could not have her at home but would help her sort something out. We were out that day, and on our return we found that Rachel had made her own arrangements. She was going to stay with a Christian family in Reading and be supported by their church! Rachel had been writing regularly to the lady, Beverley, for some time. She had herself been through similar difficulties and happened to work for Freedom in Christ Ministries. Beverley had been encouraging Rachel to visit her for some time now, and in her desperation Rachel had decided to accept the invitation. The following day she was picked up by car and driven to Reading by Beverley and her husband, Paul.

I was amazed at their willingness to take Rachel into their home, and their church's willingness to support them. Did they really know what they were taking on? During the week, Rachel received several hours of help and counselling. She was then taken through The Steps to Freedom and helped to understand what the Bible says about our true identity in

Christ. Rachel had given her life to Him in her early teens, but had lost her way hopelessly during her years of illness.

Underlying her problems and difficulties was a lie she believed about herself. She thought her body was dirty, disgusting and vile, and deserved to be harmed. The helpers at Reading showed her from the Bible that she was forgiven, cleansed and a new person in Christ. She was encouraged to identify and renounce areas in her life that were wrong and to accept God's truth. It was then that she was able to grasp just how much God loves her. She was consequently set free from all her addictions! She did not return to the CRU. The staff there couldn't understand what had happened to her, and kept her room open for six weeks in case she needed it. Rachel stayed in Reading for nine months and received ongoing help and support. She worked in the church coffee shop, helped in the Freedom in Christ office, attended an Alpha course and made lots of new friends. Rachel sounded different and looked different. She was radiant. The bandages were taken off and cuts and burns were allowed to heal. She also began to cut down on her sleeping tablets with the help of her GP, and began to enjoy her food.

Rachel sent me a lovely text message at that time. It said, "I'm better, Mum! My body is beautiful in the eyes of God, whatever the size."

Praise God; He had renewed her mind and her thinking.

We have often been asked what caused all this to happen to Rachel. It is not possible to put it down to any one thing. Rachel was in hospital in a plaster cast owing to a dislocated hip for much of her first three years. This experience may have left her feeling different from other children. However, she was a happy child, and her developmental milestones were normal. We moved house when she was eleven and she found it hard to make new friends. About a year later she had the awful experience of being seriously sexually assaulted in our own home. This might significantly account for her attempts at trying to cleanse herself in various ways. At senior school she did not get on with teachers, was a rebel and was often in the head teacher's office. She was constantly told off for misbehaving and tended to do things in order to be accepted by her peers. When Rachel left school at 16 she did a BTEC course in health studies and it was during this time that her problems really began to surface.

The past ten years have not only been traumatic for Rachel, but extremely difficult and stressful for the rest of the family. Her younger brother and sister, Andy and Sue, can't really remember Rachel being well. Sue has had to deal with extremely difficult situations beyond the experience of her years when on her own with Rachel. Rachel often confided in Sue, asking her not to tell us something, and then Sue had the problem of breaking that confidence when Rachel's life was in danger. There were also many times when I could not cope with a particular situation any more and Sue would step in and take over for me.

Looking back over the past ten years we can see how God wonderfully upheld us all. There were so many friends and family members praying for us daily and we are so grateful to them for their love and support, especially at those times when we just did not know how to pray ourselves. We were often up with Rachel on a Saturday night and into the early hours of Sunday morning and we thank God particularly for His help for David, who is the pastor of a church and was involved in taking two services on Sundays.

We give all the praise and glory to God for His hand of protection on Rachel and for His help and strength to family members. We have such a great God with whom nothing is impossible. Life has been transformed since Rachel was set free. She has had to learn to walk in her freedom. There have been many setbacks and temptations along her path to recovery, but she has learnt how to look constantly to God for help and strength to overcome. She has certainly experienced what the Bible says in John 8:32: "Then you will know the truth, and the truth will set you free."

Rachel's story

"I hate food, I LOVE FOOD.
I don't want food, I DO WANT FOOD."

1994
"What do you reckon, navy blue or black?" asked Sandra, as she looked through the rails of jeans. We were in BHS and we both wanted a new pair of jeans. I looked across at Sandra with envy – she was picking up a size twelve to try on and here was I picking up a fourteen. She was so much taller and thinner than me. I looked around; most people were taller and thinner. I was a short lump of fat – just a blob.

We got to the changing rooms. As I slipped off my old jeans I saw a fat stomach, fat legs... "What can I do?" I thought. I'd tried diet after diet, but could never stick to it and always ended up bingeing. It seemed hopeless. As I pulled up the size-fourteen jeans I could see that they weren't going to fit. I pulled them right up, and then tried to make the two sides meet. "I don't believe it!" I strained and strained. My face went bright red and my fingers hurt with the force. I couldn't breathe in any more. It was no good; they weren't going to do up. "Stupid jeans," I thought. But it's not the jeans, it's me. I'm massive, I must lose weight, I must, I must..." A real panic came over me. "I'm just getting bigger and bigger. The more I diet the bigger I get"... It wasn't the first time I'd felt this sudden panic. I had felt it many times.

Fear of food/Love of food

During the next few years I developed anorexia. I was nursing at the time, but the weight was dropping off rapidly. Some days I just couldn't face people and couldn't even answer the phone let alone leave the front door. I became unreliable about attending work. Other times I'd do six night shifts a week at the hospital even though I hadn't eaten for weeks. On our breaks the other nurses would eat, but I'd just chain-smoke. I looked at them as if they were pigs for eating and felt superior to them because I could work with no food but they had to eat. I suppose I felt I had "one over on them". But the thinner I got, the fatter I felt. At one point I was too frightened even to put milk in my tea, let alone eat anything. For example, when I was in the eating disorders unit, I'd sit in front of a plateful of dinner and just stare at it. I sat there and played with it until it got cold. As the staff forced me to eat I'd cry and cry and argue with them that it was too much and would make me fat. Other times, food was my release. I'd eat and eat for an hour and a half and then make myself sick. This gave me a sense of comfort, though I can't explain why. I was so mixed up inside. I was scared of food yet I also loved it.

Food

Food is my control
I have no control
Food holds me captive
I'm a prisoner of food

I can't live with food
I can't live without food
It holds me tight
And won't let me go

I hate food
I love food
I don't want food
I do want food

I want to be normal
With no fear of food
Food holds me captive
I'm a prisoner of food
                                    Rachel

Clubbing

I used to go clubbing three nights a week and would walk home in the early hours of the morning. On one occasion I was violently raped at knifepoint in a multi-storey car park. "That's what I'm on earth for, then," I thought. "I was sexually abused at age twelve and now raped. So that's what my body is for." I was convinced of this so I continued to go clubbing for the following reasons: to get drunk, to dance, to get hold of drugs and to be abused. Even though I felt I deserved to be raped over and over again, underneath I was scared of someone I thought of as "him". He kept getting me in my sleep when I had nightmares night after night, but I still went out looking for abuse. At this time I was taking a vast quantity of tablets a day, including tranquillisers, painkillers, laxatives, diuretics, caffeine pills and also any street drugs I could lay my hands on...

1998

I was scared of myself – scared of the voices dominating my mind. "He" was getting me. I was on my own in the house – on my own in the world. God was there somewhere, but I was mixed up in so much deception that I didn't feel able to come to such a holy God when I'd fallen so far. The darkness became darker as the feelings of self-hate welled up inside me. The cold silence and loneliness of the house was like a picture of me inside; as I walked towards the kitchen a sense of relief rushed through me.

I couldn't empty the cupboards of food quickly enough. The comfort of food didn't last long, though. After three hours of bingeing and vomiting I still felt just as bad. There was no way out now. If I cried for help, I felt as though it was thrown back in my face by people who told me I was just attention-seeking: so I had to pretend I was fine. I felt trapped. I'd never get better because I couldn't admit I needed help any more. What do I do? The feeling of despair was so strong that I started cutting my arm. This gave me a few moments of pleasure but the cuts had to be deeper and deeper. But deeper and deeper was never deep enough. I needed to see more blood – loads of blood.

"I deserve it; it's all my fault!" I said out loud as I cut all the harder. The darkness was really overwhelming me as I started crying. I can't find words for the despair I was in. I had bald patches on my head where I'd pull clumps of hair out because of the mental pain I felt deep within. Even if I had cuts from head to toe it wouldn't be as bad as how I felt inside. It was mental agony.

Screaming

I'm screaming inside
Its all dark, and I can't see
I'm scared
But I know he's there
Haunting me
Hurting me, trapping me

I'm crying for help
But no one's there
No one
I can't do it myself
I need help
Someone, please, help me.

My inside hurts so much
I can't numb it
But I can't relieve it
He's always there
Haunting me
Hurting me, trapping me

No more – please – no more
Someone hear me
Please
No one can hear me
But I'm screaming
Screaming.

Rachel

1999

"...You do not have to say anything, but anything you do say may be given in evidence later on in court..."

I often heard this sentence, and then would find myself in a police car on the way to the police station. On one occasion I was so high on drugs that I was cracking jokes and I asked if I could try on one of their police hats.

Later, locked in a cell for hours on end – that was when despair would take over. The walls of the cell were made of stone; there was a metal toilet pan and a mattress with no cover and being only four or five stone in weight I was freezing cold. I cried and screamed but got told to be quiet. Hours and hours of loneliness were ahead of me. There was no way I could get out. But even if I was out – what would be the difference? I was a prisoner, whether I was in a police cell or not. I was living a life of slavery anyway.

I was stripped naked by female officers while they checked for drugs. Had they examined me internally they would have found what they were looking for. Then a doctor came to check that I was fit for interview. On the occasions when I had been arrested for prescription forgery, the doctor would be really horrible to me. After that came the interview. I watched as the interview cassettes were opened and put into the machine. I was never nervous during an interview. My life was such a mess anyway that I didn't care what happened. Sometimes after being released, I'd find myself being arrested again within a couple of hours. I would be taken back to the police station where I would go through the same formalities. Following my release I would go back to town and do the same things all over again.

I remember one time in court I stood there while the magistrate spoke. I felt faint, and I ached because I weighed so little. At one point when sitting I slid and dropped my bottle of water. I was so weak that I couldn't hold it. Some court officials came rushing to see if I was all right – the magistrate told me to sit up straight. "Sit up straight?" I was far too weak to sit up at all. "No one has any idea," I thought... On this occasion I was given two years' probation.

Back at the police station they took my fingerprints and my photo was taken while I held up a board with my offender's number on it. "So what?" I thought. "I don't care any more. I'll be dead soon anyway. The world is against me and I hate myself. No one cares and I can't wait to be dead."

May 2000

I woke up in intensive care with tubes coming out of me everywhere. I looked to my left: there was Sister Sutherland (the night sister I used to work with). "You silly girl" she said. I tried to answer and that's when I realised that I had an airway in – I was on a life support machine! "How long had I been here? What had I done? Why hadn't it worked?" and the biggest panic of all was "I'm still alive! Why do people keep stopping me from dying? Why can't they just let me go?"

It wasn't until days or weeks later that I realised what I'd done. I'd taken a large quantity of antidepressants after cutting myself – and I'd been shouting and screaming at Dad: that's all I could remember. Then apparently I'd been having epileptic fits in A & E. I was then sent to intensive care on life support. I would have died that night if Dad hadn't taken me to A & E. I felt totally trapped. Why couldn't anyone let me die?

Trapped

I'm trapped
I can't see out
I can't see how to get out

It's dark
There is no light
It seems forever
Please let me out

I'm stuck in here
Everyone else is outside
Enjoying life, having fun
I just can't get out

I can't move
I can't see
I want to be outside
Please, God, save me

Rachel

December 2000 onwards

In a period of twelve days I'd been rushed to hospital four times by ambulance and every time I got home again I ended up back in A & E. On the fourth occasion Mum and Dad said they couldn't cope with me at home any more. And the doctor at A & E said that if I left the department they would call the police again. I was admitted into the psychiatric ward at the local hospital again, this time for eight months, and after that I was admitted to a Crisis Recovery Unit in London. Hospital became my home. A nurse followed me around wherever I went. I was watched in bed, in the bath, in the toilet, and lost my dignity completely. What I now realise is that these nurses saved my life by following me and watching me in this way. But I certainly didn't appreciate it at the time!

What nobody saw

I'd lie on my bed at night crying so hard that it hurt. The agony inside was beyond words. I was lonely and frightened. Wherever I went people would see me drunk or drugged, thin, pale, looking withdrawn and miserable. But that's all they saw. They didn't see the inside – the pain, the terror, despair, crying for help but unable to receive it. But this still doesn't explain properly – still doesn't explain the utter despair, darkness and hell that I was in. Weird though it may seem, the only comfort I felt was the sense of evil around me. Freddy had me.

Freddy Krueger

He was an evil character out of the horror movie called *Nightmare on Elm Street*. This Freddy had an orange-and-green stripy jumper, a hat, a very evil-looking face, and, worst of all, four knives for fingers on one hand. I used to watch horror movies all night every night at one time, but this particular one had a significant hold on me. In the movie Freddy would go around slicing people with his four knives when they fell asleep. I have four deep scars on both legs and on one arm, which I was convinced Freddy had done and not me. Freddy was always in the right-hand corner of the ceiling in my bedroom. I could see him as clearly as I saw anyone else. I used to be so frightened, but nobody knew.

Satan told me that if I didn't offer my blood for him Freddy would get my soul. So I cut myself and drew off blood with a syringe, collected it in bottles and offered it to him in rituals. The evil presence in my room gave me a buzz. At least someone was there. This still doesn't fully express how horrific it was. Psalm 88:18b applied to me at those times – "the darkness is my closest friend"...

If I fell asleep, the rapist and Freddy got me. If I stayed awake, Freddy and Satan got me. Drugs and drink were my only answer. With these I escaped reality. I became detached from everyone else and the world around me – lost in my fears and wishing to be dead. Yet each time I tried to kill myself, I survived.

Fear

I'm frightened
I'm frightened of the future
I'm frightened by my past
And I'm frightened at present

The fear is so real
So strong, so overpowering
It haunts me day and night
And is always there deep down

My inside is in knots
Full of anxious thoughts
My head is in pain
Exhausted by these thoughts

I'm frightened of the day
I'm frightened of the night
Please, God, give me comfort
In place of this throbbing fear
Rachel

Last resort – Drugs

"Rachel, what is that toxic smell – like burnt plastic?" asked my sister, Sue, as she walked into the house.

"It's my bubble bath", I replied.

A few minutes later she suddenly shouted at me, "Rachel, what on earth is the kettle doing in the microwave? And why are you wearing my shoes?" Mum and Dad were on holiday at the time. My brother and sister had been out and I was so drugged that I'd become totally confused.

I had overdosed on a type of sleeping pill that can be bought over the counter and which had become my last resort at times when I could not get hold of prescription or street drugs. Chemists started refusing to sell it to me, as they could see I was buying countless packets each week. So I'd shout at them and knock down shelves, and on one occasion I grabbed a batch of ten packets and ran! That is how desperate and addicted I was. Late one evening I left the gas on the hob unlit.

My mum, sister and brother took me to hospital because I was very drugged.

"Rachel, what pills have you taken?" asked the nurse in A & E. "Um... antidepressants, um... sleeping tablets, um... cabbage, peas... um carrots..." I replied.

"Have you taken anything else?" asked the nurse.

"I've written the cheque and I'll bring it to college tomorrow," I replied.

"Did you leave the gas on at home?" asked the nurse

"Yes," I said.

"Don't you have an electric kettle at home?" she asked.

"Well we did, but I put it in the microwave!" I replied.

I don't remember saying any of this but was told afterwards, and this confusion was a result of three packets of this drug. I did many other dangerous things while on this drug. I set the cooker on fire, threw my pet mouse over the garden fence, put my cat in the birdcage, talked to the toaster, wrote a cheque to "two cheeseburgers" instead of my brother, and generally talked complete nonsense. My drinking, drug addiction and self-harm grew worse, and my eating habits were all over the place. I was living in a totally different world from everyone else and I was at my wits' end.

Agony Inside

> *Oh the pain*
> *Where does it come from?*
> *Why won't it go?*
> *I don't know*
>
> *Such intense agony inside*
> *Makes me want to die or hide*
> *I just can't bear it*
> *It's too much*

The pain is deep, deep inside
No one can see it
But I can more than feel it
Deep, deep inside

Please leave me alone
When will it end?
Is there an end?
Oh the pain...

Rachel

So where was God in all this sorry story? Was I aware of Him at all? Perhaps I should say at this point that I had, some time earlier, begun to look for positive help and had gone to stay with a lady who had been through something similar. In her home I received prayer and counselling and was later encouraged to read some of Neil Anderson's books. I did improve for a time after this, and even managed to do some hospital work, but, sadly, I gradually slipped back into addiction again. Now, several years later, I felt I had hit rock bottom.

Then suddenly my life changed dramatically, and the change came about in a really remarkable way. While in the CRU I was so ill that I poured boiling water all over my hand and arm. This was the most painful form of self-harm I had ever inflicted on myself and I was doing it on a daily basis. I damaged myself in ways I don't even want to go into. I was also on large amounts of laxatives most days. I was abusing diuretics and any other drug I could get hold of.

On the unit we had to report any self-harm within hours. During a weekend's leave I had overdosed and did not report it until I got back to the unit. I was told I had to take a week's instant leave as a punishment for this, and had to find somewhere to go immediately. Mum and Dad felt unable to cope with my illness any more and could not take me back. I felt abandoned, rejected and unloved. Where could I go? In a state of utter despair and desperation, I telephoned someone who worked for Freedom in Christ and who had been writing to me for the past year. I took her by surprise when I asked her if she would put me up there and then, but she agreed to come and get me and her church agreed to support her and her husband as they helped me. I was in a really bad state and was severely drugged, my arms in extensive bandages, and I was starving myself. I felt trapped and suicidal. I felt that my life was out of control. I was in the hands of the evil presence that materialised before me regularly from the horror films I had watched and who made me do the things I had done. I felt like there was no way out.

But Beverley took me into her home, cared for me and began to take action. She arranged for me to go through The Steps to Freedom in Christ at the end of the week. On the morning of this appointment, as I sat in the room, Freddy was up in the right-hand corner as usual. I thought, "I'll do or say what these two ladies tell me and then I can at last go back to the CRU and start cutting my face." But, no, God had other plans – quite the opposite, actually! As I was taken through the Steps and renounced the evil, my self-harm and everything else, I could see that the smile on Freddy's face was gradually going and he started fading away. By the end of the eight-hour session, the darkness had totally disappeared from the room and from my presence. God had set me free – completely free!

I had become aware that I am a precious child of God, totally loved, accepted and secure in Him – so why did I need all my old coping mechanisms when I can rely on Him alone for my strength? Also, I realised that my body belonged to my heavenly Father, and the desire to hurt it had now gone! I burst into fits of laughter at this point because of the overwhelming joy that had come flooding into my soul! I'm accepted, I'm secure, I'm loved, and I'm His beautiful child.

How amazing! After this, Beverley helped me to understand "stronghold busting" and showed me how to take thoughts captive when I felt threatened by the enemy. Her love and support were there for me while I was still learning to walk in the freedom God had given me. Looking back, I say – humanly speaking – how did my body survive those years? But God had His hand on my life, because every time I tried to kill myself I puzzled the medical staff by surviving. Because God wanted me here – to live for Him and help others, which is what I am doing now. Those ten years seem like just a very bad dream. I had no idea what I was missing out on: the joy, the peace – because I've got my Jesus! The freedom, and the overwhelming sense of thankfulness that I now have something I can never lose because I'm secure in Him.

One night after I had been set free, I went to bed but could not sleep. Every time I shut my eyes I saw myself running and Freddy was behind me, chasing me. He kept reaching out and ripping my clothing with sharp knives – but he couldn't quite reach me and he kept falling over. This was God showing me that Satan will try to trip me up, but he can't actually reach me because I'm running the race with Jesus! On another occasion I was being tempted to drink, and when I shut my eyes I saw a curtain and one of Freddy's knives tearing through it. I felt that this was a warning from God that, if I went down that road, Satan could creep back into my life. "No way!" I thought, so I told him where to go and spent some time worshipping God instead!

During the nine months after my freedom appointment I stayed in Reading learning to renounce any lies from the enemy or temptations as they came. This was a real struggle at times, but Beverley, Jane and their helpers never gave up on me. They also found activities for me to help me get used to living a normal life again.

The day came when I finally felt ready to move back home

with my family. Since then I have been learning how to live "a life of worship", and God has blessed me beyond words. I'm back at my church and feel a real part of it instead of isolating myself like I used to. It's a wonderful church to be in: they're my spiritual family and I love them.

I have also gone back to nursing and am thoroughly enjoying it. But most of all I've got my Jesus, and I could never go back to how I was before. I love Jesus so much and want to live my life for Him. Yes, I've had my struggles, but I praise God for struggles – because they make me stronger in Jesus. If it had all been easy, I wouldn't have learned to fight. I was set free, but had to learn to walk and live in that freedom.

[Praise God, he] heard my cry! He lifted me out of the slimy pit, out of the mud and mire; he set my feet on a rock and gave me a firm place to stand. He put a new song in my mouth, a hymn of praise to our God. (Psalm 40:1–3)

It could happen in your church

Despite the fact that Rachel's problems seemed so profound, she found her freedom in a local church with the help of people who were not experts. I am full of admiration for those church leaders who took a step of faith and were prepared to welcome a complete stranger with difficult issues into their midst, and especially for Paul and Beverley, who took Rachel into the heart of their family with all the risks that involved. Lest you think they were equipped with a huge house and plenty of time on their hands, let me tell you that they both work, have two young children with all the usual needs for school runs, homework and taking to activities, and have no room in their home for a long-term guest. They converted their dining room into a bedsit for Rachel while she was with them.

Whyever did they put themselves and their family through that? Because they knew from personal experience that Christians with troubles like Rachel's do not need to stay in their apparently hopeless situation but can see those difficult issues resolved in Christ as others help them along the way.

Yet, although she would probably never have made it without the sacrificial help she received, the real credit for Rachel's walk into freedom lies with Rachel herself. Ultimately, she is the one who chose to believe the truth even though it did not seem true at the time. She is the one who chose to forgive. She is the one who chose to close the door to the enemy's influence in her life. Most of all, she is the one who goes on making a choice every day to believe the truth and reject the lies that the enemy throws at her. No one else can do that for her.

I had a personal connection with Rachel's story in that one of my own staff had taken her into her home. However, I (and Freedom in Christ Ministries) had very little direct input into Rachel's recovery other than to support those who were helping her. Helping captives find their freedom is the work of the local church. The role of an organisation such as Freedom in Christ Ministries is simply to support, equip and encourage local leaders as they engage in the God-given mission of the church to set captives free and make disciples.

I am aware that reading a story in a book can make it seem remote; detached from your own daily life. There is an understandable tendency to think, "That could never happen to me", or, "We could never help people like that in our church". Think again! Every single one of the people you will read about in this book is a very ordinary person just like you and me. That's especially true of all those who helped a hurting person find their freedom. None of them has any "special anointing" or "unique gift". However, they do all have something much better than that – they have "life in all its fullness"! If you're a Christian, you have it too – and that's what makes all the difference.

The consequences of Adam and Eve's sin

To understand this, we need to go back to the Garden of Eden and take in the almost unimaginably devastating consequences of Adam and Eve's sin, already helpfully outlined for us by Neil Anderson in his foreword.

When God created Adam and Eve, He gave them not only physical life but spiritual life as well. This meant that they enjoyed a number of very important benefits: an intimate, personal relationship with God; real significance; complete acceptance; absolute security. They didn't know what it was to have a need. They had been given purpose in life: to rule over the earth. We too were designed for that kind of life.

They didn't realise what they had until they lost it. God warned them that, if they ate of a certain tree in the garden, they would die. Well, they did eat. Did they die? Not physically (at least not for 900 years) – but they did die spiritually. The consequences of this were severe. They were cut off from God. They lost their significance, acceptance and security. They suddenly felt alone in a world they couldn't control.

What has that got to do with you and me? Because of their sin, every one of their descendants comes into the world physically alive but spiritually dead. We were designed to have a relationship with God, not to have to worry about needs, and to have a purpose. But we were all born into a very different environment from the one God intended for us.

The only possible answer to that predicament is to restore our relationship with God, to become spiritually alive again. That was not something we could accomplish ourselves. So God sent Jesus to undo the works of Satan who had deceived Eve, resulting in the sin that separated her and Adam from God. Jesus died in our place and took our sins upon Himself to make it possible for that relationship to be restored.

It's about life in all its fullness

If I were to ask you "Why did Jesus come?", what would your answer be? I would hazard a guess that most Christians would say "To forgive our sins" – and, of course, that's true. But look at where Jesus himself put the emphasis:

> I have come that they may have life, and have it to the full. (John 10:10)

Dying for our sins was a means to an end: to restore to us the life that Adam and Eve lost. We needed Good Friday but it would have had no meaning without Easter Day, the day of the resurrection, the day of new life.

> I am the resurrection and the *life*. He who believes in me will *live*, even though he dies. (John 11:25, our emphasis)

In other words, he will live *spiritually*, even if he dies *physically*. What Adam lost was life. What Jesus came to give us was life.

> He who has the Son has life; he who does not have the Son of God does not have life. (1 John 5:12)

Many have come to think that eternal life is simply something we get when we die. In fact it's much better than that – it's a whole different quality of life *right now*. It's simply getting back the life that Adam lost at the fall. The moment we received Christ, our spirit was reconnected to God's Spirit – we were spiritually born again.

This is not just some theological concept. A very real and profound change took place deep inside you when you became a Christian. Paul says in 2 Corinthians 5:17: "... if anyone is in Christ, he is a new creation; the old has gone, the new has come." You might have the same body as before, perhaps even the same thought patterns, but the truth is that deep down inside where it really matters you have been completely transformed. You have changed from being someone who was by nature an object of God's wrath (Ephesians 2:3) to someone who now shares God's divine nature (2 Peter 1:4). Deep down inside you are now spotlessly clean and very, very nice! Through the grace of God, you have received back the very life you were always meant to have.

This is the reason that the Gospel really works. Having the life of Christ within us makes it possible for us to get back to the position Adam and Eve had before the fall. This life in all its fullness is what makes it possible for you – and for any Christian – to resolve the negative effects of the past and move on. It means that we have the same significance, security and acceptance that Adam and Eve had before they sinned.

That you have this new life if you are a Christian is a fact. However, the issue for freedom is knowing the truth – "You will know the truth, and the truth will set you free". If we don't know – really know – that we have the life of Christ within us, and what that means, then the chances are we will probably not behave very differently from before.

For example, many Christians do not feel at all secure, significant and accepted. Yet the Bible is clear that we are now all three. Here is a list assembled by Neil Anderson of the things that the Bible says about us regarding our significance, security and acceptance, put into a series of "I" statements. Many Christians have found that simply reading this out loud every day for a number of weeks while committing themselves to believe it has made a significant difference to them. Why not try reading it out loud now? Bear in mind, however, that the issue here is not so much how you read it but whether you are prepared to believe what God says about you rather than what your past experiences and circumstances have taught you to believe:

Who I am in Christ

I am significant

I am no longer worthless, inadequate, helpless or hopeless. In Christ I am deeply significant and special. God says:

- Matthew 5:13, 14 – I am the salt of the earth and the light of the world.
- John 15:1, 5 – I am a branch of the true vine, Jesus, a channel of His life.
- John 15:16 – I have been chosen and appointed by God to bear fruit.
- Acts 1:8 – I am a personal, Spirit-empowered witness of Christ.
- 1 Corinthians 3:16 – I am a temple of God.
- 2 Corinthians 5:17–21 – I am a minister of reconciliation for God.
- 2 Corinthians 6:1 – I am God's fellow worker.
- Ephesians 2:6 – I am seated with Christ in the heavenly realms.
- Ephesians 2:10 – I am God's workmanship, created for good works.
- Ephesians 3:12 – I may approach God with freedom and confidence.
- Philippians 4:13 – I can do all things through Christ who strengthens me!

I am secure

I am no longer guilty, unprotected, alone or abandoned. In Christ I am totally secure. God says:

- Romans 8:1, 2 – I am free for ever from condemnation.
- Romans 8:28 – I am assured that in all things God works for my good.
- Romans 8:31–34 – I am free from any condemning charges against me.
- Romans 8:35–39 – I cannot be separated from the love of God.

- 2 Corinthians 1:21, 22 – I have been established, anointed and sealed by God.
- Philippians 1:6 – I am confident that the good work God has begun in me will be perfected.
- Philippians 3:20 – I am a citizen of heaven.
- Colossians 3:3 – I am hidden with Christ in God.
- 2 Timothy 1:7 – I have not been given a spirit of fear, but a spirit of power, of love and of self-discipline.
- Hebrews 4:16 – I can find grace and mercy to help me in time of need.
- 1 John 5:18 – I am born of God and the evil one cannot touch me.

I am accepted

I am no longer rejected, unloved or dirty. In Christ I am completely accepted. God says:

- John 1:12 – I am God's child.
- John 15:15 – I am Christ's friend.
- Romans 5:1 – I have been justified.
- 1 Corinthians 6:17 – I am united with the Lord and I am one spirit with Him.
- 1 Corinthians 6:19, 20 – I have been bought at a price. I belong to God.
- 1 Corinthians 12:27 – I am a member of Christ's body.
- Ephesians 1:1 – I am a saint, a holy one.
- Ephesians 1:5 – I have been adopted as God's child.
- Ephesians 2:18 – I have direct access to God through the Holy Spirit.
- Colossians 1:14 – I have been redeemed and forgiven for all my sins.
- Colossians 2:10 – I am complete in Christ.

Suggestions for further reading

The main Freedom in Christ teaching is contained in two books:

- *Victory over the Darkness* (Anderson, Monarch, 2004)
- *The Bondage Breaker* (Anderson, Monarch, 2004).

Alternatively, you can go through the Freedom in Christ Discipleship Course, available as:

- *Leader's Guide* (Anderson & Goss, Monarch, 2004)
- *Participant's Workbook* (Anderson & Goss, Monarch, 2004)
- DVD-Video series (Goss, Monarch, 2004)
- Tape series (Goss, Freedom in Christ Ministries, 2004).

All are available from your local Christian bookshop or directly from Freedom in Christ Ministries.

Chapter 2

We already have everything we need

As I write, it is three years since Rachel found her freedom, and she continues to move forward. She was sharing her story one day when she said, "I was stuck in anorexia for ten years and then suddenly God set me free!" I had to say to her, "Was it really like that?" The hard truth is that she could have taken hold of her freedom at any time in that ten-year period. God was not waiting for a particular moment to act. He had already done everything He needed to do.

Like many others, Rachel was waiting for God or somebody else to do something, to fix her. The answer came when she did something herself, based on what had been done for her already by Jesus.

When Paul prayed for the Ephesian church, what did he pray? That God would give them more power... that God would give them more blessings?

As you read his prayer for them, ask yourself for each item whether it refers to something that has already taken place or whether it refers to a future event:

> I keep asking that the God of our Lord Jesus Christ, the glorious Father, may give you the Spirit of wisdom and revelation, so that you may know him better. I pray also that the eyes of your heart may be enlightened in order that you may know the hope to which he has called you, the riches of his glorious inheritance in the saints, and his incomparably great power for

us who believe. That power is like the working of his mighty strength, which he exerted in Christ when he raised him from the dead and seated him at his right hand in the heavenly realms, far above all rule and authority, power and dominion, and every title that can be given, not only in the present age but also in the one to come. And God placed all things under his feet and appointed him to be head over everything for the church, which is his body, the fullness of him who fills everything in every way. (Ephesians 1:17–23)

Some of Paul's prayer is future-oriented. He asks that they will receive the Spirit of wisdom and revelation and that their hearts will be enlightened. Why? So that they will connect with what has *already happened*: the hope they already have; the power they already have; the amazing blessings they already have. He also emphasises strongly the position that Christ already has, which is the basis for what we have because we are seated with Him in the heavenly realms.

In fact, if you read any one of Paul's letters, you'll find that he spends the first half of it emphasising what has already happened, what we already have in Christ. Only then does he move on to give instructions on what we should do in future.

Consider these two key verses and pay special attention to the tenses:

His divine power has given us everything we need for life and godliness through our knowledge of him who called us by his own glory and goodness. (2 Peter 1:3)

Praise be to the God and Father of our Lord Jesus Christ, who has blessed us in the heavenly realms with every spiritual blessing in Christ. (Ephesians 1:3)

You already have everything you need for life and godliness. You already have every spiritual blessing in Christ.

If you asked me to name one thing that characterises all the defeated Christians I have met, it would be this. They don't know what happened to them when they became Christians and the amazing consequences that follow from that. They have completely missed the point! They are concentrating on how they want things to change in the future when, in fact, the answer comes when they realise what has already happened in the past. There is nothing more for God to do. The missing ingredient is our response to Him in repentance and faith.

Rachel's problems stemmed from the lie she believed (due to past experiences) that she was dirty. Connecting with the truth that, despite her past experiences, she was in fact a pure, clean child of God made all the difference. It was knowing that same truth that set Jason free to turn from his addictions to become a fruitful disciple.

Jason's story

"By the time I entered college, I had tried almost every drug with the exception of heroin. Every weekend and holiday was just another party..."

When I look back over the years, I still find it amazing to realise how much my life has changed. The person I am now bears no relation to the pathetic character I had become. To be living what many would call a "normal" life is in itself a miracle, and one for which I shall be eternally grateful.

For years my life was that of a miserable drunk. I did not see any way out, and I was told by my friends – and even by doctors – that I would probably die a drunk.

When I was 22 I thought I had arrived. I had just finished college and started work as a graphic designer. I was also newly married to a woman I had met at college, and we had just bought a new apartment together. Little did I know that this would become my prison for the next six years. But how did it all begin?

I was born in Toronto, Canada in 1970. My parents met at art college and, through my uncle, had met some interesting folk who were known as "Children of God". My parents went along to the coffee houses to hear their songs and testimonies, and soon both made a commitment to the Christian faith. After this they joined the group, and the following years were spent travelling from city to city, country to country.

Growing up in this environment was exciting for a young child, but inevitably brought with it a certain amount of instability. My brother and I were taught at home by our mother, and it was a lonely existence. As the years progressed, the teaching of the "Children of God" became more and more perverted, and my parents, by the grace of God, began to feel uneasy. They realised that much of what they heard was not of God and that they were actually involved in a cult. Settling back into Canadian life took many years, as my parents were naturally very wary of churches and schools after their experiences with the "Children of God".

We finally settled back in Toronto in 1980. By this time there were six of us children – two girls and four boys. It was not the best of neighbourhoods, as we were surrounded by drug dealers. My parents took us to church and daily shared God's word with us. However, over the years the influence of my friends, both in the neighbourhood and at school, began to win me over. By the time I entered college I had tried almost every drug with the exception of heroin. Every weekend and holiday was just another wild party. I thought this was the normal way to live, and that a Christian life was just too extreme and too rigid. I followed what those around me did, not wanting to look out of place. I would say one thing and do another.

All the same, I considered my life to be more or less normal – until I fell in love. Marriage seemed to offer so much of what had been lacking in my life – intimacy, friendship and the security of a really meaningful relationship. But, two months into the marriage, disaster struck. My wife set off for work one day and informed me that she would not be returning. I was devastated. I could not figure out what was wrong – after all, we had only just got married. Our life together had hardly begun. She denied that there was anyone else involved, and said that she just needed to "sort things out in her life". However, I later found out through a mutual friend that she had started an affair three months before the wedding – with a man at her workplace who was already living with another woman.

I felt utterly destroyed. I turned to drink immediately – all I had built my life upon had crumbled in a day. I managed to keep on working but every free moment was spent in front of a bottle. It became my only friend, because as the years passed by friends slowly left, as they could not take my depressing attitude any longer. As my drunkenness increased, I began to suffer from severe depression. I became suicidal, but my belief that in God's sight suicide was wrong forced me to carry on.

My parents moved out east to the province of Nova Scotia, not knowing about my alcoholism, as I had somehow managed to hide it from them. But before they left they introduced me to a man who was to have a profound influence on my life. Mike ran a small design firm and, more importantly, he was a Christian. I started doing part-time work for him and he would gently speak to me about matters of faith. I had by this time been drinking for about three years and it had become the centre of my life. All my money went on supporting my habit.

Slowly, over the next few years, I started attending a church. I began to read and study the Bible afresh. I started to realise that it was not just the drink that was ruining my life but a host of other problems I hadn't even considered. I tried Alcoholics Anonymous and drug programmes, but always gave up. Everything seemed too much and I could see no way out of my lifestyle. Then a small miracle happened. The firm I had been working for went bankrupt and Mike offered to take me on full-time. The people who worked at the firm were all Christians, and proved to be a great source of encouragement. But I kept everything hidden from them, as I thought I was too sinful to be really accepted by them. Sometimes it was a struggle to make it through the day. I suffered panic attacks and many times would simply fall asleep from sheer exhaustion. But as soon as I had a drink everything seemed possible, and those few moments of bliss seemed worth all the misery it caused.

During this period of my life I finally made a commitment to God and was baptised. However, my resolve quickly crumbled again as I tried as always to do it in my own strength. Finally, as the debts mounted and everything fell apart, I told Mike about my problem. He kindly, but firmly, gave me two options: get help or get out. This is tough love. Strangely enough, I also received another job offer at the same time, but realised that I had no skill left and that even if I took the job I would not be able to keep it. I grudgingly allowed my church to get me help. They were wonderful. They all pulled together, helping me to do up my home and put it on the market. They offered no condemnation – only love.

The place they had arranged for me to go was Teen Challenge. I had never heard of it before, and was quite sceptical about the programme. I thought I was already a Christian, so what more was there? The answer, as I would later learn, was discipleship. When I arrived, I was accosted with hugs and constant greetings of "He loves you, brother". I thought they were all nuts – or, worse, that I was back with another cult.

However, deep down I knew that this was where the Lord wanted me to be. It was a totally different environment from any that I had ever been in. The centre was located on a farm outside London, Ontario, and waking up each morning to the smell of fresh manure was something that took some getting used to! The regime was very strict but I made a resolve to finish the programme, especially as my home had now been sold and I had nowhere to go. I felt as if I was starting all over again.

During the programme we read *The Bondage Breaker* by Neil Anderson. As I read this book, the teaching it contained began to break into my heart and mind. I realised that this was just what I needed to help me come to terms with my past life, and to deal with it. I laid everything before the Lord. Alcohol, drugs, sex, violence and the evil thoughts that had wrecked my life. I took all these, one by one, and laid them at the foot of the cross. No more could the devil, or my own conscience, bring them again before me and accuse me. They were dealt with at the cross.

It was like the moment in *Pilgrim's Progress* where Christian's burden falls away at the foot of the cross. I had been set free, once and for all, because of what Jesus had done when He died for me, paying the penalty for all the mistakes I had ever made.

The simple but profound message that has stayed with me is "Who I am in Christ". This is a list of all the things that the Bible says about my identity as a Christian. These are powerful ammunition against the thoughts that, especially during the first year, come to attack you and remind you of all your past sins. The enemy starts whispering his lies in your ear, telling you how worthless you are, and how you mean nothing to anyone – not even to God... That is when you need to "take the shield of faith, wherewith you shall be able to quench all the fiery darts of the wicked (one)" (Ephesians 6:16,

Authorised Version). I began to put my heart into everything and really can say now that it was the best year of my life.

Nearing the end of my year, I still did not know what I would do. But one day the director came up to me and told me they were going to send me to London, England. I was overjoyed! I had never told anyone, but it had always been my desire to go to England. By means of yet another small miracle, the amount of money I had made on the sale of my property exactly equalled my debt, which left me free to transfer to London, England.

I have been working for Teen Challenge for the past four and a half years, and have loved it. When I arrived they had a new computer waiting, and needed lots of different jobs to be done, from logos and brochures to building a web site. I have also met a wonderful woman named Liz, who has been a great source of joy and companionship. We are now married and it is just fantastic. I am so grateful to be given a second chance at life. Liz has been able to accept me for who I am *now*, and does not judge me for my past.

This is another important truth I have learned: no matter what is in our past life, if we accept Christ as our Saviour, then we are a new creation. When God looks on us He doesn't see our sins but sees His Son, who died to set us free. I look forward to each new day with a joy and a hope that is only to be found in our Lord and Saviour, Jesus Christ. He has promised that if we delight ourselves in the Lord, He will give us the desires of our heart. If we commit our way to Him and trust in Him, He will do this (Psalm 37:4–5).

By His grace, these promises are daily being fulfilled in me!

We are saints

In our teaching sessions, I often ask an audience how many of them have grown up thinking they are "forgiven sinners". Most hands go up. Well, they certainly were sinners and they certainly are forgiven, but, in the New Testament, it is unbelievers who (over 300 times) are identified as "sinners". Believers, on the other hand, are identified (over 200 times) as "holy ones" or "righteous ones" or "saints" – and never clearly the other way round. If you have received Jesus as your Lord, you are not a forgiven sinner but a redeemed saint!

That's not just a title. It reflects the fact that at the moment you became a Christian – even if you're not absolutely sure when that moment was – you became a new creation in Christ. Your very nature – who you really are deep down inside – changed from being someone who could not help but displease God to someone who is accepted, secure and significant in Christ.

One lady put it to me like this: "I used to think of myself as a filthy dog with a white coat on. I knew that I was covered by the righteousness of Christ but deep down I still believed that I was an abomination to God. Now I'm starting to realise that I've actually become a clean dog!"

A lot of us can identify with that. I certainly can. Galatians 3:27 says that we have clothed ourselves with Christ. Many of us have come to think in effect that we're still the same dirty, rotten, no-good people underneath – just that all that is disguised because we are clothed in Christ's righteousness. An analogy may help: when the prodigal son returned home, he was given the best robe to wear (Luke 15:22). But was it the robe that made him a son? No. He was given the robe *because* he was a son. We are now righteous through and through.

This is not to do with our salvation. It's about our behaviour. If you see yourself, as Jason did, as a miserable sinner, how will you behave? Like a miserable sinner. But if you see yourself as you really are – a holy person dearly loved by a heavenly father who welcomes you into His presence even when you mess up – then you have a chance of living a holy life.

If you want to change your behaviour you have to see yourself as more than just forgiven. Nobody can consistently behave in a way that is inconsistent with what they believe about themselves.

Wendy, too, experienced her freedom when she realised the wonderful truth about who she is in Christ.

Wendy's story

"As a full-time mother, I wanted so much not to repeat the mistakes of my own mother..."

I suppose my problems began pretty early on in my life. Although I was brought up in a loving, God-fearing home, I often felt sad and lonely as a child. It was as though I had no hope, and nothing seemed to make me happy. Life seemed futile somehow and I longed for things to be different. I had one brother and my parents were quite strict with both of us. I am sure they did love us, but somehow they seemed unable to show us that love in any way that had meaning for us.

I was always consciously trying to be good and to do what they wanted, for fear of being punished. My mother often seemed to be irritated with me. I think she resented the fact that she had to stay at home; she often said that she was just an unpaid servant! She was by nature a perfectionist and very controlling. If you wanted any praise or affirmation you had to do things her way.

On one occasion, when I was about six, I decided to do the washing up and tidy the kitchen as a surprise for her. I was sure she would be really delighted. I was so disappointed by her reaction, and the memory has stayed with me over the years. My mother *was* pleased, but then she proceeded to tell me that I had not quite done the job properly: "If a job is worth doing it is worth doing well," she said. I felt crushed and angry and in my heart I vowed that I would never do anything like that for her again.

I think it was in this way that I came to believe the "lie" of perfectionism: there is no point in even attempting something unless you can be certain of success. Not only did this bring with it a great fear of failure, but I also felt that my worth as a person depended on what I managed to achieve.

When I was twelve I became a committed Christian, and this was such a source of comfort and joy to me. I knew that God loved me, but as I still could not really comprehend what unconditional love was all about I felt that I had to do great things for Him in order to gain His favour. So it was that after university I went into full-time Christian work for six years. This included working among Muslims in North Africa for four difficult years.

When I came back to the UK I went into teaching – not the best kind of job if you are a perfectionist! And I had not really anticipated how much time I would need to spend on marking and preparing work. Because of my own very high standards I found that practically all my time went on these things, and before long I became very depressed and emotionally vulnerable.

So when a colleague at school – a non-Christian and a womaniser – began to pay me attention, I found it hard to resist. I knew it was wrong, but I ended up getting involved with him. It was a terrible time; my life began to fall apart as I oscillated between cutting myself off from him and then getting involved again. I saw a Christian psychotherapist for a while and this helped me to see a few home truths more clearly. I realised that a poor sense of my own self-worth was at the root of my erratic behaviour.

Many of my friends were praying for me as I went through this struggle and by God's grace I managed to break free from this relationship. Within a year – amazingly – I met the man who was to become my husband. This was a really happy time as we settled down to married life and planned to start a family. But despite my husband's love for me I continued to suffer with feelings of worthlessness and depression. I was dismayed to find that this became worse after I had our two children. As a full-time mother I wanted so much not to repeat the mistakes of my own mother. I did not want to put the demands of running the home before showing my love and care for my children. Somehow this proved to be incredibly difficult, and I often wondered if I was achieving anything at all, the old sense of being a failure beginning to haunt me again.

A friend at church who knew of my struggles suggested that we meet to pray. She told me about the Neil Anderson books and suggested I had a look at the "Steps to Freedom" booklet. We spent a whole evening praying through the Steps together. This was a turning point in my life.

The next day was absolutely amazing. I had lived all my life with condemning voices in my head telling me how worthless I was and inciting fear and depression within me. But on the day after we prayed together there was a beautiful silence. No voices of condemnation; just joy and a wonderful sense of being accepted and loved. Straight away God began to change patterns of behaviour that had clearly stemmed from my feelings of worthlessness. Now I can invite people around to the house without the nagging fear that they will find me untidy! This new-found freedom from worry about how the house looks has also freed me to enjoy my children more, and to be able to spend more time with them.

I am learning to accept that I am a different person from my mother. I may not have her particular skills and abilities but I have gifts of my own, and it is up to me to use them. I have started having piano lessons again, as I enjoy them.

These are a valid source of fulfilment for me even though my parents may not see why they are important to me. I feel free from the constraints of perfectionism that had previously dogged my path and prevented me from doing things; I have even begun to write articles for the church magazine – and enjoy experimenting with new recipes in cooking as well.

I know now that my personal worth is not bound up in what I do or what I achieve; it has its source in the love of Christ for me. That is where my true value lies. Zephaniah 3:17 has become very special for me – a wonderfully liberating promise:

> The Lord your God is with you, he is mighty to save. He will take great delight in you, he will quiet you with his love, he will rejoice over you with singing...

Who could ask for anything more reassuring?

Again, Wendy's story emphasises the crucial importance of knowing who we now are as Christians. Most of us know what it is like to struggle with doubts about our self-worth and self-image. In fact, in a world that measures people according to what they have, how they look or what they achieve, it would be difficult for any of us not to struggle with these matters. The breakthrough for Wendy came when she went through The Steps to Freedom in Christ.

Let's look again at one thing she said: "I had lived all my life with condemning voices in my head telling me how worthless I was and inciting fear and depression within me. But on the day after we prayed together there was a beautiful silence. No voices of condemnation; just joy and a wonderful sense of being accepted and loved."

My favourite verse in the Bible is Romans 8:1: "Therefore, there is now no condemnation for those who are in Christ Jesus." To be honest, I was puzzled by it for a long time. It clearly said that there was no condemnation for me if I was a Christian – and I was – yet that did not tie up with my experience. I felt condemned all the time! I now realise that there is no condemnation from the only person who matters – God Himself.

There is, however, plenty of condemnation from other sources. Satan is not called "accuser" for nothing – he accuses us before God day and night – and other people often condemn us too.

I still suffer from feelings of condemnation. However, I have learned that I can simply ignore them. If God is for me, who can be against me? (Romans 8:31)

Suggestions for further reading

- *Overcoming Negative Self-Image* (Anderson & Park, Regal, 2003)
- *God's Power at Work in You* (Anderson & Saucy, Monarch, 2003)
- *Unleashing God's Power in You* (Anderson & Saucy, Harvest House, 2004).

Available from your local Christian bookshop or directly from Freedom in Christ Ministries.

Chapter 3

The Steps to Freedom in Christ

If it were just a question of having someone tell us about our new identity and our instantly grasping the implications of it, it would be relatively easy. However, it's amazing how many Christians have been told for years that they are "new creations" but simply do not connect with that truth and its implications in any meaningful way. They believe it at one level but it doesn't go much beyond head knowledge.

I've lost count of the number of times people at our conferences have found that it's suddenly fallen into place and have said to me something like, "I just wish someone had told me all this 30 years ago". On a couple of occasions they have been with their pastor and I've seen exactly what's been going through their pastor's mind: "I've been *telling you* for 30 years!"

Why is it that it's possible to want to move on with the Lord, to sit listening to excellent teaching in churches, to read inspiring Christian books, yet for our lives to remain very little changed? Jesus said that it was knowing the truth that would set us free. But simply telling people the truth doesn't guarantee that they will know it.

Merely trying harder isn't enough. In fact the answer has always been the same: repentance and faith. But what do those things really mean?

Faith is simply believing that what God tells us is true. The problem is that our past experiences and the world around us have taught us to look at life in a way that doesn't reflect reality. For example, when the Israelite army was cowering at the prospect of one of them having to do the apparently impossible and defeat the giant Goliath, a young boy came along, marched boldly out towards the giant and killed him. The army saw the giant in relation to themselves whereas David saw him in relation to God. Whose view reflected reality? David's! Walking by faith means bringing our belief system into line with what is already true, and acting accordingly.

Repentance too is something we sometimes struggle with. The Greek word *metanoia* means "a change of mind". It's a radical change of perspective, turning away from past sins and learning to think differently. Many of us have come to Christ but have not been taught how to repent.

We have seen from those who have shared their stories so far that a key part of their healing came when they went through The Steps to Freedom in Christ. It's a process that helps us to repent and to commit ourselves to the truth in God's word.

It's time to take a look at what The Steps to Freedom in Christ are and how they work.

Kay's story

"John and I spent every spare minute together, and soon I came to rely completely on him for everything. He was my world – and he knew it..."

I had a pretty normal childhood, and have some happy memories of my home and school life. But when I was fifteen years old my parents decided to move house and I had to change schools. We then moved from the town where I had lived for seven years to a small village. No one at my new school lived in the same village as me, and as I had no opportunity to meet other teenagers I became isolated and lonely. For two years I pined for my old life and for the friends I had known at my previous school. Then, suddenly, everything changed.

I met a guy who completely swept me off my feet. He bought me flowers and gifts and took me out for meals and on lots of exciting day trips to various cities, or to the coast. Life became colourful and romantic. It was just wonderful to be free of loneliness and boredom. I was no longer stuck at home with nothing to do and no friends to talk to. John and I spent every spare minute together, and I soon came to rely completely on him for everything. He was my world – and he knew it. Before long he began to take advantage of my dependence on him, his attitude towards me began to change, and he started to abuse my trust.

Eventually I realised he was lying to me. He would stand me up and make up some completely false story about where he had been. I became very insecure and possessive and to my horror we were soon having terrible rows. There came a day when I told him that I had had enough, and that I would rather be on my own than living the kind of life that ours had become. But as I tried to leave he blocked my way, grabbed hold of me and began shouting abuse at me. As I struggled to free myself he suddenly lashed out angrily and hit me. I was horrified. This was the end...

But I could not break free from him, and this became the pattern of our relationship over the next four years. After he had been violent, he would always be incredibly remorseful. He would turn up at the house in tears and shower me with gifts, making the inevitable promise that he would never do it again. I tried to stay strong and keep away from him but he would harass me until I gave in. I didn't know how to escape him. My family gave me little support and in those days I did not know Jesus as I do now, so I had nowhere to turn. I felt completely trapped.

One day I met a lovely Christian man through work. His name was Mark and we began to go out together. Surprisingly enough, once he knew I was with someone else, John accepted that our relationship was over, and he left me alone. I came to know the Lord through Mark, and was able to confide in him about my violent relationship with John. For years, however, I felt unable to tell anyone else about it, because I felt so embarrassed and ashamed. I was sure everyone would think me weak and stupid for allowing myself to be treated so badly.

Unfortunately, my violent past affected my relationship with Mark. We got married, but I found it hard to give in to him when issues arose over which we could not agree. I never wanted anyone else to have control over me physically or emotionally again. If Mark tried to assert his authority over a decision we needed to make, a great anger would well up inside me. My heart would pound and I would end up feeling shaky and nauseous. I would fly off the handle, and we had huge rows during the first few years of our relationship. Things did improve a lot as I came to know the Lord better, and as Mark and I came to know each other better. Mark learned not to make snap decisions but to talk things over, and to treat me more sensitively.

The church we attend offers everyone the opportunity to go through The Steps to Freedom in Christ. I looked into this and knew deep down that this was what I needed to do. But I still felt unable to share about my past and my previous violent relationship. It was still very painful, and I could not get rid of the feeling of shame and deep embarrassment. Whenever I had tried to tell anyone about it before the words just would not come out. But now I found that writing it all down was a great relief and a very real help in giving expression to those dark memories.

When I went through The Steps to Freedom with my encourager, I found that I was now able to discuss it all with her. I had an overwhelming sense of freedom in just being able to admit it all to someone else, and then to give it to God.

For the first time in ten years I knew I had been released from the sense of shame I used to feel about what I had suffered.

All that welling up of anger that I used to feel had gone. I now feel happy and secure in my relationship with Mark. I am able to submit to him when that is needed and we hardly ever argue any more. By keeping close to the Lord, and following the teaching laid down in His word, I have come at last to real fulfilment and happiness in my life.

Kay reports that just one session had the effect of releasing her from ten years of shame. Is there something "magic" about The Steps? Is there some kind of unique gift from God or anointing on Freedom in Christ Ministries and those who use its approach? Of course not.

The Steps to Freedom in Christ is just a tool, a structured way to help people assume their responsibility to repent, to submit to God and to resist the devil. The Steps don't set anyone free. It is Christ alone who sets us free as we respond to Him in repentance and faith.

How do The Steps work? If we have done something that is spiritually harmful, we open a door to the enemy to have some degree of influence in our lives. Ephesians 4:26–27 gives an example of how this works:

> **"In your anger do not sin": Do not let the sun go down while you are still angry, and do not give the devil a foothold.**

Anger itself is not sinful – it's just an emotion – but if we don't deal with it in short order it turns to bitterness and we give the devil a "foothold". That word for "foothold" is *topos* in Greek, which literally means a "place". It's the same word Jesus used when He said He was going to prepare a "place" for us.

Simply becoming a Christian does not automatically remove those footholds. We need specifically to renounce each one and The Steps is simply a tool to help us do that. Renouncing past activities that have opened the door to Satan's influence in our lives is a critical part of repentance. Ever since the earliest times, the church has encouraged new Christians to declare: "I renounce you, Satan, and all your works and all your ways". Most traditional church streams still do that but many newer streams do not. In our experience that renunciation needs to be applied as specifically as possible.

As we clear out the "rubbish" in our lives in this way, we close the doors to the enemy and our minds become clearer so that we can really know the truth that will set us free.

Lisa struggled for 25 years with some very serious problems. The Steps to Freedom was the key to her recovery and she helpfully describes the process for us in some detail.

Lisa's story

"I knew I needed a very special kind of help but I didn't know where to find it..."

I was born into a loving Christian home. I had one sister, two years younger than myself, and we lived in our own terraced house in a small market town. When I was seven years old, my father felt called to be a pastor. We sold up our home and moved to London, where we lived in rented rooms while my father went to college to do his training. Later we moved into a manse in the heart of the country, and settled down to a completely different way of life.

When I was twelve, a tragedy befell our family. My sister became very ill and after a year of various treatments and stays in hospital she died. During this time my parents tried to protect me from what was happening, which meant that we never discussed it. I went to stay with friends at the time of my sister's death, and was not asked if I wanted to go to the funeral. Secretly I felt confused and excluded.

Things never seemed the same again after this. I knew my sister was in heaven but I felt overwhelmed with a deep sadness. I could not even imagine what my parents were feeling, but no one seemed to want to talk about it. I knew they were being upheld by their faith, and I tried desperately to feel the same.

I did know Jesus, because at the age of nine I had asked Him into my heart. We had a guest speaker at a mid-week children's meeting in our church, and the things that he said really touched me. I realised for the first time that Jesus had actually died on a cross for my sins and that He wanted me to ask Him into my life. I said a prayer that night in bed, but did not think much about what I had done until a few years later, when I was at secondary school. I had been given a Gideons New Testament at this school and I found a page at the back, which invited people to sign their names if they wanted to commit their lives to Jesus. I felt I was ready to do this and later, when I was 17, I asked for baptism. Our church practised baptism by immersion, and my father was delighted to baptise me alongside a lady who was 70 years old!

A year later, at the age of 18, I left home to do my nursing training. Taken from a sheltered family background into a busy hospital, I soon found my rather shallow Christian life challenged. I let go of many of the principles I had been taught to hold dear, and allowed my life to be taken over by the world I now inhabited. Gradually my new lifestyle began to erode my previous standard of living. Because I was often working on a Sunday my attendance at church became spasmodic; usually I only went if I was home for the weekend. I didn't read my Bible, and I didn't pray unless there was an emergency. I had quite a lively social life, and made some good friends at the hospital. But I had some destructive relationships as well. An affair with one of the doctors led to disaster and I had a termination of pregnancy, which I kept a secret from everyone. Least of all did I want my parents to know, and it was several months before I actually told them.

This was the start of 25 years in and out of depression, during which time I struggled to find my way back to Jesus, and to the peace I had lost. At 25 years of age I had to leave my job and go back to live with my parents because I could no longer cope with life. Various people tried to help me but eventually I was referred to a psychiatrist. I spent long stretches in psychiatric hospitals, had electric shock treatment many times, was permanently on prescribed antidepressants, and life became one long struggle.

On occasions I would get back to work for a couple of years or so and then end up back in hospital. Things got so bad that I was in utter despair. Death seemed to be the only way of escape and I ended up trying to commit suicide. I was fed up with antidepressants, with their accompanying side effects. But I was also racked with a deep sense of guilt, and conscious of unforgiveness in my life. Eventually I became very frightened and unapproachable, cutting myself off from everybody who tried to help me. I knew I needed a very special kind of help but I didn't know where to find it. I came out of hospital at the end of the year 2000 determined to get my life put right.

"Alpha" courses were taking place at our church, and although I had thought previously that these were not for people who were already Christians, I felt so broken that I decided to join, seeing this as a means of renewal. In doing this, I was unaware of all the prayers that had been going up on my behalf and which were now being answered.

It was from this point that things began to fall into place. Steve Goss from Freedom in Christ Ministries came to our church and talked about how other people had found their freedom in Christ, and mentioned that a course entitled "Finding your Freedom in Christ" was due to begin in a nearby town. I decided to join. The Alpha teaching had been a great blessing, but I knew that I needed something more. I needed to be set free from all the things that had held me in bondage for so long. As we were shown what freedom in Christ meant from a biblical point of view, hope began to blossom. I started to read Neil Anderson's study books and we were given Bible verses to memorise. We also listened to testimonies from people who had been released from all kinds of bondage. I was determined that this would be my experience, too, because I now recognised that many of my problems had a spiritual root. I knew that Jesus was the only one who could sort out my depression and heal my broken life. He was the best psychiatrist, and He alone could set me on the right road again.

There came a time when I felt ready to ask for what was called a "one-to-one" appointment. For this, one needs to set aside a day to meet with two Christians who lead you through seven Steps to Freedom in Christ. One of these two people does the actual leading while the other person is there to give prayer support. I felt immediately comfortable with my two helpers, and we spent about five hours together, stopping for lunch and tea breaks. With God's help I was able to cope with all this and knew that each thing was being dealt with as we prayed.

The seven Steps are: Counterfeit versus Real; Deception versus Truth; Bitterness versus Forgiveness; Rebellion versus Submission; Pride versus Humility; Bondage versus Freedom and Curses versus Blessings. Some of the Steps were more meaningful to me than others, but they all had some relevance. As I read the verses of Scripture and spoke prayers aloud, I knew that I was on the verge of a new life of freedom.

In the first step we dealt with the occult, severing any connection I had had with this realm. Secondly we dealt with ways I had been deceiving myself – or allowing Satan to deceive me – by living in a fantasy world or by blaming others for things that went wrong. I saw that, while truth is the revelation of God's word, we need to acknowledge the truth in our inner self. Psalm 51 became very relevant here.

Next I was told that we need to forgive others and Ephesians 4:31 and 32 came into play here. As we prayed through this, I named anyone I had not forgiven, and felt the wonderful release of having been forgiven myself. I saw how these two aspects of forgiveness are linked together and how Satan cripples us with a sense of guilt when we do not forgive. I began to see how Satan had gained a foothold in my life, and how I had become a victim of his taunts and accusations.

The subject of rebellion followed next, and I saw how I had thought my way to be the best way – better than the ways I had been taught as a child. I had to pray that I would learn to be submissive to God and to His word. Pride was the next enemy we had to face. I saw that I had been more of a people-pleaser than someone who wanted to please God, and that I needed to humble myself. I was reminded from Proverbs 16:18 that pride goes before a fall!

The next step dealt with bondage to sin, and I learned from Scripture how I could be completely set free and begin life with a clean slate. We went through ways in which we get ourselves into bondage through sexual sin, and other pitfalls. Then the final step dealt with family ties – things that had happened in the family through generations. These things needed to be severed through the power of the Holy Spirit's action, and we prayed that they would no longer have any power over me. Exodus 20:4 and 5 were the verses we read here.

Throughout all this I was conscious of God's help. I knew that each new thing was being dealt with as we read the relevant scriptures and prayed our way through. Afterwards, at the end of the day, I felt as if a great weight had been lifted from me. I knew that I had found the freedom that I had longed for and which had eluded me for so many painful years.

The next thing was to learn to walk in freedom and to keep close to the Lord. My antidepressants were cut down, although my doctor would not take me off them completely. I hope one day I might be allowed to live without them, but I have to remember that there is a history of depressive illness on my father's side of the family, so I must keep close to the Lord and trust Him to help in this area of my life. I have overcome on the forgiveness issue, and must keep free in this area, praying each time old thought patterns try to return. I now realise how important daily reading from the Bible and regular times of prayer are, as well as a conscious effort to fill my days with things that are pleasing to God.

Now I am finding fresh opportunities to serve God, and in so doing I am gradually gaining the self-respect and confidence that were once completely lacking in my life. I now know who I am in Christ. I know that He has redeemed me and set me free.

When you go through The Steps to Freedom, you simply ask the Holy Spirit to bring to your mind anything and everything you have done that might give the enemy any kind of influence in your life. Of course He is delighted to show you, and many people suddenly remember things they hadn't thought of for years. It's a "belt-and-braces" exercise, an opportunity to put everything on the table before the Lord and deal with it.

Sometimes the Lord doesn't show you everything on one occasion – probably because it would be too much for you to deal with – and you can come back on a future occasion and do some more.

The importance of forgiving from the heart

It may come as a surprise to learn that, for many people, the most crucial part of the Steps process is Step 3, which deals with forgiveness. However, as Paul shows, one of Satan's primary schemes against us is to get us to remain in bitterness:

> If you forgive anyone, I also forgive him. And what I have forgiven – if there was anything to forgive – I have forgiven in the sight of Christ for your sake, in order that Satan might not outwit us. For we are not unaware of his schemes. (2 Corinthians 2:10–11)

One of Satan's greatest points of access to our lives is the sin of unforgiveness. Forgiveness is the key to freedom. Most feel, to start with at least, that what has been done to them is so enormous that they cannot possibly forgive. Two important truths, in particular, are important here.

Firstly, we need to come to the understanding that the reason Jesus commanded us to forgive is for our own sakes. Strange as it may seem, our forgiving another person has precious little to do with the other person. It's primarily an issue between us and God. Why does God command us to forgive? Because He does not want the past to control us any more, He does not want us feeling increasingly bitter, angry and unhappy, and He does not want us opening up our lives to the enemy's influence. We don't forgive for the other person's sake – we do it for our own sake. We don't have to go to the other person or let them know we have forgiven them. We simply have to go to God and make a choice to forgive.

Secondly, God does not sweep the sins of others under the carpet as if they don't matter. They *do* matter. They matter deeply. When we forgive, we are not saying that what was done was OK. It was not OK. We are simply taking a step of faith to choose to let go of our right to seek revenge. However, that is not the end of the story. God says, "Do not take revenge, my friends, but leave room for God's wrath, for it is written: 'It is mine to avenge; I will repay,' says the Lord" (Romans 12:19). When you forgive, although you are letting the other person off your hook, you are not letting them off *God's* hook. You are trusting Him to be the righteous judge who deals justly with every sin. Every single person will stand before Him and have to give an account for what they have done. Either it will be paid for by the blood of Christ if the person is a Christian, or they will have to face the judgment of God if they are not. God will settle every account some day.

Not a quick fix

Sometimes when someone goes through The Steps, the results are dramatic. However, I'm always at pains to point out that this is in no sense a "quick fix". If they have not learned how to stand in the truth, they are likely to go back downhill when the same issues arise in the future. That is why I personally never take someone through The Steps unless they have first had the opportunity to process the basic teaching about who they are in Christ, the nature of the spiritual battle and how to stand.

This postscript to Lisa's story demonstrates clearly the importance of this.

About two years after this, I had what is best described as a "blip". I was under some pressure at the time, from worry about plumbing problems in my flat.

For a couple of months depression tried to take hold of me, and I found it hard to read my Bible and pray. Things started to get out of proportion and my thinking became distorted. My GP sent someone in from the local mental health team to assess me, with the result that my medication was increased for a few weeks. For a moment, I thought I was on a downward spiral once again. Then I simply claimed the truth that I had been set free.

I looked at Neil Anderson's books again, and got in contact with a friend who had also been helped through Freedom in Christ. She gave me a special prayer to use, and some key verses of Scripture. Friends prayed for me and with me, and instead of being overtaken by depression, as I had so many times previously, my condition improved after a few weeks. Life became normal again, and I could pray and read my Bible once more. I could look back to my freedom appointment and know that what took place there had changed my life.

In the Bible it says that when two or three people meet together in Jesus' name, he will be with them. The prayers that day were answered. Satan had been vanquished and I had been set free. The weakness I have mentally can be overcome by looking to Jesus, and claiming His victory for myself. This experience has brought me great comfort.

You have nothing to lose by going through, or taking someone else through, The Steps to Freedom in Christ. All that is happening is that someone is assuming responsibility for their relationship and walk with God. Nobody accuses anyone of anything. The worst thing that can happen is that they will be really ready for Communion next time they get the opportunity!

Suggestions for further reading

For individuals who want to go through The Steps:

- *The Steps to Freedom in Christ* (Anderson, Monarch, 2004)
- The Steps to Freedom in Christ DVD-Video (Goss, Monarch, 2004).

A 21-day devotional specifically written to help you once you have been through The Steps:

- *Walking in Freedom* (Anderson & Miller, Regal, 1999)

A guide to taking others through The Steps and establishing a "freedom ministry" in your church:

- *Discipleship Counselling* (Anderson, Regal, 2003)

Available from your local Christian bookshop or directly from Freedom in Christ Ministries.

Chapter 4

The battle for our minds

It would be possible, perhaps, to get the impression from what we've looked at so far that change comes when we suddenly realise that we have not been believing truth, almost as if it's a case of just getting the right doctrine. Yet you can have the best doctrine in the world, and still not be free.

There's a major fact that those of us brought up in the West all too easily tend to leave out of the equation. From the beginning of Genesis to the end of Revelation, there's one continuous theme in the Bible: the battle between the kingdom of darkness and the kingdom of light; between the father of lies and the Spirit of Truth; between Jesus Christ and the antichrist.

Some may be tempted to think "I am a Christian so it doesn't affect me". In fact, Paul tells us explicitly that we are not fighting flesh and blood but the spiritual forces of wickedness in the heavenly realms (Ephesians 6:12) and that we need to put on the armour of God. This armour is clearly not for non-Christians but for Christians. The truth is that, in the spiritual battle that is raging, we are the main targets! Ignoring the reality of the situation leads to defeat. We are in the battle whether we like it or not, but it's entirely winnable at every stage even for the newest, most inexperienced or vulnerable Christian.

We tend to look for the activity of demons in "dramatic" episodes. But the battle takes place primarily in the mind of every believer.

We read in 2 Corinthians 4:4 that Satan "has blinded the minds of unbelievers" and the effect of footholds of the enemy in our lives seems to work in believers in much the same way. They cause a degree of spiritual blindness and make it more difficult for us to "connect" with truth. If we do not take the opportunity to deal with these footholds, the battle for our minds remains a continuous struggle.

Going through The Steps to Freedom in Christ is a gentle and controlled way of dealing with them. Many find that they are then able to get hold of truth in a way that they have never experienced before. We will always need to guard our minds and take every thought captive but, once we have resolved our personal and spiritual conflicts and learned to keep renewing our minds to the truth in God's word, the battle becomes much less intense.

Peter's story is a good illustration of the battle for our mind.

Peter's story

"I was in a band and we wrote songs about horror and the devil. The songs also disrespected Christians, but for some reason I didn't feel comfortable about being offensive about Jesus..."

I grew up in a family that didn't go to church. We were not anti-faith but we tended to have little interest in organised religion. However, as I grew up, I became intrigued by the idea of life after death, and was open to any and every theory going about the meaning of life. Christians irritated me when they said that they had the "one true way". I thought this was arrogant, and an old fashioned idea.

As a child I developed a big interest in horror films. My bedroom walls were covered in scary posters. At school, it seemed that almost every story or book review I did had something to do with horror. Sometimes the teachers would comment on it but eventually they accepted that I actually hoped to work in horror films when I was older.

I wasn't a loner; I was a happy and popular kid. At school I had plenty of friends, and did well at my schoolwork. It was just that the horror stuff was my biggest interest. Eventually, the images and ideas contained in the films I was watching started to make me curious. I began to wonder if there really was life after death, and if the supernatural was something you could experience in this life.

This sort of thinking led me to make friends with other people who thought the same way. We began to find out all we could about the occult. Once I made a Ouija board in wood-work at school, but a classmate destroyed it. My friends and I determined not to be deterred, made our own out of glass and bits of torn up paper. I used this contraption many times, either in a group or on my own. I tried out spells and séances, and anything else that I thought would be exciting. I wanted to know that the stuff in the films I was watching could be experienced in reality.

At the time I was in a band, and we wrote songs about horror and the devil. The songs also disrespected Christians, but for some reason I didn't feel comfortable about being really offensive about Jesus. This sort of thing went on for years, with my friends and I going on ghost hunts and making our own cheesy horror films with a home video camera.

Although all this stuff was exciting and fun I did have a few frightening experiences, but I still kept coming back for more. Despite all this activity, I was really very normal. Interest in the paranormal was very "accepted" during the time I was growing up. It was not a case of a stereotype situation, with a kid who feels rejected, dresses like a Goth and is into creepy stuff. But although I remember my teenage years as a happy and fun time, it was also a difficult time for my whole family, owing to the fact that my mum and dad got divorced. However, for some reason I thought it would be best for me to "put on a brave face" and bury my emotions. It seemed like a good idea at the time. It wasn't.

It was when I went to university that I started to think more deeply about the meaning of life. I went to join the occult society, but didn't have enough money that day, so I joined the science-fiction society instead! At the end of the first term I met a Christian girl who invited me to the Christian Union. I had recently felt myself getting more and more open to Christians. And as I was seriously attracted to this girl, and wanted to go out with her, I agreed to go to the Christian Union.

Meeting all these other young people who were Christians was a definite eye-opener. The more I heard about the Bible, and the more I read it, the more I became convinced that there was definitely something in this Christian stuff. But I put off making a commitment because I felt I could never be good enough. It was a while before I realised that this wasn't the point. I finally saw that it was *because* I wasn't good enough that Jesus had to die. The meaning of the cross gradually became clear to me, and after a lot of discussion and reading some books on the subject, I went for it and became a Christian.

My life now changed in a big way. Over the next year I found myself in a genuine relationship with God and it affected my behaviour and relationships with others. The change was very dramatic and many people were amazed at how I'd been transformed – shocked even! I certainly wasn't perfect but I was definitely a new person.

When I had been a Christian for about a year, I began to realise that there were issues in me that had not been dealt with. Some of this was emotional baggage related to growing up through my parents' divorce and not really dealing with it; some was to do with my having messed around with Ouija boards, etc. and my obsession with horror films. Gradually I realised that I had problems that needed to be sorted out.

I decided to go and see a minister in the town where I was at university and he advised me to get some Christian counselling. He said that he sensed there was some evil around me that was trying to influence me. This seemed a little freaky, but part of me liked it. It felt exciting. Some of the attraction to this whole area of horror and evil was still there and I knew I needed help.

I went for the recommended counselling and found it very helpful. I felt under spiritual attack at some points. But at the same time I felt that things were getting cleaned out. At the end of that time, I met the minister and the counsellor and they asked me to name and repent of each one of my previous activities – things that I knew had offended God. This process marked a real turning point in my life, and made a big difference to my Christian experience.

However, looking back, it was in some ways like getting a fresh coat of paint. I felt better and cleaner, but I couldn't see the problems under the surface. I hadn't really grasped anything about my new identity in Christ. I felt as if there was a tug of war going on for me between God and Satan, and although I knew myself to be in "God's camp" I knew that something wasn't right. I felt confident that I was going to heaven and that I was a Christian, but part of me was haunted by a feeling of insecurity about who I was deep down.

I felt guilty about almost enjoying the "evil" experience and it made me think I must be a pretty weird Christian! Occasionally I'd be walking along and suddenly get a really horrible image in my mind. This was probably a memory of some scary film I'd seen way back. But for a while I was scared of the dark as well. I would see this black shape in my room, coming towards my bed. I knew that, in spite of all the tremendous changes that had taken place in me since becoming a Christian, I was still weak and vulnerable in this particular area.

After university I joined a Christian band and we toured for a year, going into schools to talk about Jesus. I felt close to God during this period, and was really rejoicing in being a Christian. But I still got jumpy around Hallowe'en. When I saw horror stuff in the windows, I felt myself being drawn towards it. I wanted to go back and look at the masks, or see the latest Hallowe'en posters. I ended up getting really condemning thoughts. I knew I shouldn't be into all this stuff. What was wrong with me?

There came a day when, on tour in a certain town, I felt this compelling thought that I should go and throw myself in the river. I had never been suicidal and this was really weird. Weird – yes – but, at the same time, part of me was almost feeling excitement. My life had indeed changed in such a major way that I started thinking that maybe, deep down, I was basically a strange person.

I knew that some of the friends back in my home town, who were still involved in the stuff I used to do, had been badly affected by it. One of the guys who used to do the Ouija board with me went to prison, and I remembered on one occasion talking him out of killing himself. Anyway, he ended up committing a really sick crime. When this happened it affected me badly. It brought all sorts of feelings of guilt and confusion and made me realise that I could have ended up like him.

Although things improved for me after a while, there remained a little niggling worry in my head that I might be a bit of a freak. Once or twice while I was driving I had the thought of driving off the road. Maybe I should make it clear that I never seriously considered doing these things, but just the fact that such a thought could enter my head alarmed me.

I'd say to myself, "Whoa, you're a psycho if you can even *think* like that!"

I knew my future with God was secure; I never doubted my salvation. But I would feel that there was a battle going on in my mind and I was going to have to put up a good fight if I was to prevent myself from becoming a product of my past behaviour. Although the negative thoughts came only occasionally, I was deeply uneasy about them. I knew I'd done a lot of inner cleansing when I prayed with the minister those years before, but I also knew I had not internalised what it means to be a "new creation".

I had originally joined the band because I wanted to serve God through music, but during the year I had found the work with young people really rewarding. After touring with the band for a year I had made some contacts in a church that was looking for a youth pastor. After a lot of prayer and consideration I went for an interview, and was offered the job. I then moved from the north to the south of England, started the new job, and also got married to the very same girl who had invited me to the university CU all those years before!

Looking back, I am constantly amazed by the way God has been at work in my life – even planning that the person He had set aside to be my wife and companion in His work should be the one to lead me onto the Christian path in the first place. He certainly makes sure that "everything works together for good for those who are called according to his purpose". And that promise from Romans 8:28 is only one of the many that have been fulfilled in my life. I may have failed Him many times but He has never failed me.

While working as a youth pastor, I went to Spring Harvest with my youth group and heard about some seminars run by Freedom in Christ Ministries. The other seminars going on that first day didn't appeal to me, so I decided to give the Freedom in Christ stuff a try. Over the next few days I was blown away. It wasn't exactly that anything particularly powerful happened. I mean, there were no voices from the heavens, or even a sense that God was nearer than usual; it was just a logical and quiet discovery of what had already happened when I first became a Christian. Nothing had changed except my perception of who I was.

I went through The Steps to Freedom, and as I did so it reminded me of what I had done years earlier with the help of that minister while at university. That was a very important way of cutting off the connection with the past, but what really took hold of me during the Freedom in Christ seminars was the teaching; I went away realising that the old me was gone, that my future was not based in or bound to my life before I met Jesus: I was someone totally new! When I heard about the battle for the mind in which Satan engages as his tactic against Christians, things took on a whole new perspective. This was not a tug of war any more between God and the devil, with me in the middle. I was sorted with Christ, once and for all, pure and simple. All I had to do was to keep on the alert for any lies the devil fired my way and go on living as the child of God I truly was.

Since then, my walk with God has taken on a whole new perspective. I know that at my very core I am a saint, and that knowledge makes it more natural for me to live like one. When I sin, I know that it does not suit me any more. If a bizarre thought pops into my mind, I take it for what it is: just a poor little attempt by the devil to make me think that I am not a "good Christian". And anyway, since I acquired my new perspective, that kind of thought has stopped.

The Freedom in Christ approach is the most significant breakthrough I have ever had since becoming a Christian. And the cool thing about it is that, basically, all it has done is to explain more fully what actually happened to the essential "me" when I first acknowledged my need and asked Jesus to become my boss and best friend. I have discovered my true identity in Him.

Even though Peter was in church leadership, there was a battle going on for his mind. He went through The Steps, closed the doors that had been open to the enemy, and a lot of the teaching he'd heard for years fell into place.

However, just going through a repentance process such as The Steps is not the whole story. Early on in his Christian life, Peter had been taken through such a process but had not been able to identify wrong thought patterns and work on them. In the same way, it's perfectly possible to go through The Steps and end up free, but spiral back down to where we came from if we are not aware of the battle that's going on for our minds and don't do some work to renew our old ways of thinking.

Suzanne's story further illustrates the battle for our minds and shows how even the most sincere Christian can find him- or herself being led astray by the enemy.

Suzanne's story

"To my horror, I felt God was telling me to go and live on the streets of Liverpool without any money and with just the clothes on my back..."

The only reason for writing my story down is that I want to share with other people something of what God has done in my life. The story begins way back in childhood, which was on the whole a happy one. We were what I suppose would be called a normal family. I had two sisters, a mother and a father, and life seemed to run pretty smoothly for us all. I was quite a popular child; yet in spite of this I always felt myself to be inadequate compared to other people. I never felt I was funny enough, good-looking enough or confident enough about anything.

As I became a teenager I just could not seem to handle the way my body was changing. Deeply unhappy about the way I looked, I started to diet. Soon I was losing weight yet could not control what was happening to me; I started to drink heavily and stay out late at night. By the time I was 21 my life revolved around my experiences of getting drunk and sleeping around. Deep down I was yearning for love and attention. Yet at the same time I felt that I didn't need anyone at all. I had no real relationships with boys – just sexual ones. I was sinking into a state of denial, but could do nothing to prevent my gradual deterioration.

When my mother became a Christian I must have been about thirteen. I remember mentally rejecting the whole idea of God; my mother's new experience of Him left me feeling alienated and cold. Then when I was 22 things began to change dramatically. I had just lost my job and felt very low. I had been drinking and had actually taken an overdose. Desperate now for help, I told my mother what I had done.

I saw shock and horror register on her face for a moment. Then something extraordinary happened: my mother began to pray for me, pleading with God to touch my heart. And suddenly I heard myself telling her that I wanted to become a Christian. It was a very precious moment that I will never forget.

After this I started to go to church. But inside I still felt very inadequate. I had expected to make friends now that I was joining in with a church fellowship. But close friendships still evaded me, and after a while I lost interest and went back to my old ways.

It was a few years later that I met someone very special. He was everything I'd ever dreamed of – good-looking and easy to get on with. We moved in together and for a while things were smooth-running and we were happy. But there came a time when my partner seemed to grow distant and uncommunicative. In spite of my doubts we actually got engaged and planned to marry the following year. After this things began to improve, and he once more became loving and attentive.

Everything was going well until I received a phone call from a girl who claimed that she had been seeing my boyfriend for over two years. I was devastated. I confronted my boyfriend and he eventually told me the truth. He had met her at work. He said they had become good friends and then things had just developed into something more. I just did not know where to turn. I got on my knees and asked God to help me. I didn't want to let go of David, but I knew I had to. I moved out of the house and returned to my parents' home. I had never known such pain and sorrow – yet God had a purpose in it all because it led me back to Him.

I started attending church again and moved in with two Christian girls. My life seemed to be getting back to normal again but I still felt lonely and empty inside. I started a new job in a supermarket, behind the meat counter. I didn't really enjoy it but I needed the money. I still felt very isolated because I didn't see very much of the girls I was living with. Somehow I sensed that I couldn't really talk to my family about the way I felt either.

For no apparent reason I began to "fast" regularly. Somehow it seemed to make me feel high, and I told myself it would make me feel closer to God. But as time went on I became more and more isolated. I would go to work then come home and listen to worship tapes all night long in a desperate attempt to change how I felt about myself. I now had no life outside work and church. I was so intense about God that there was no room for anything else in my life. Somehow I felt that if I put everything into God then nothing would harm me.

By this time I had started to see a counsellor and was taking antidepressants. This helped for a while but then I started to get an uncontrollable urge to fast again. I was convinced that God was telling me to fast for three days without water or food. And I felt He was saying that this was for a pretty important reason. Friends warned me against this but I would not listen. I then asked God why I had to do it, and to my horror I felt He was telling me to go and live on the streets of Liverpool – without any money and with just the clothes on my back.

So one morning I just left, without telling anyone where I was going or why. I had told the pastor's wife the evening before what I was thinking of doing. She just couldn't believe it, and did her best to dissuade me. I don't think she believed I would actually do it. The next few months were like a dream. When I look back now it just does not seem real. I was literally living on the streets day and night. I would also stay in hostels every now and then. I thought that if I went home God would punish my family and me. It was a living nightmare for them and me and I can't bear to think now what it must have done to them.

I also felt that God was telling me to fast again while I was on the streets. I felt that it was my mission to tell everybody about God. I see now that His protecting hand was on me all through this time and I am deeply grateful that He brought me through it.

I was eventually taken into a psychiatric hospital but not before I had jumped into the River Mersey, convinced that God was telling me to do it. At the time I was sure this was my punishment for not fasting for long enough. The voice that was telling me to do this led me to believe that God would rescue me in the river, as He did with Jonah. I stayed in the water for a bit, then decided to get out. Someone sent for an ambulance and I was taken to hospital to be checked over. I now realise that the river episode was Satan's plan to get rid of me.

It was to take another two years of hell before I realised

how deeply the enemy was deceiving me. I had been having trouble sleeping and I constantly heard voices telling me that I was going to die. I had horrible nightmares and dreaded going to bed. I just felt I couldn't take any more – and nor could my long-suffering parents. The next three years of my life were spent in and out of hospitals, but nothing seemed to help. I went on fasting and feeling more and more desperate and depressed. I felt I had let God down as well as everybody else. The house group I sometimes attended decided to fast and pray for me for a month to see what God would say. And this was when the miracle happened.

It was the Saturday evening of the first week of the fast. My mother had suggested that I should read a book by Neil Anderson called *Victory over the Darkness*. I decided to flick through it and see how I felt about reading it. Then I came to a part about a girl who was having similar problems to mine – she was hearing voices telling her she was going to die. Neil Anderson, who was counselling her at the time, told her that it was Satan who was feeding her these lies.

As I read, it was as if a light had been switched on in my mind. Could *I* have been listening to Satan all this time, thinking it was God? It took a while to sink in, but gradually I realised that I had been deceived all those years. I felt very strange at first. I went through a range of emotions, especially anger – which was mainly directed at God. I suppose I just couldn't understand how a loving God could let this happen to me. I now realise that it was my own pig-headedness that got me into the mess I was in. I unknowingly allowed Satan to take over my mind and my life. Gaining access through all my negative emotions, he eventually began to control me.

God amazingly stepped in at the right time and He knew when I was ready to accept the truth. I had to come to the end of myself before I would listen. I now realise that God was with me all the time, but I would not listen to Him or to other people. I had been listening to the wrong voice all the time; Satan wanted to destroy me and he knew how vulnerable I was. During the next few months he continued to harass me. I was still feeling depressed so my doctor put me on antidepressants. These helped in some ways but I still felt very down.

Then, one day, my house-group leader told me about the book *The Steps to Freedom in Christ*. She told me she would go through it with me if I should decide to do it. So I looked through the book and decided to go ahead with it. We worked through The Steps on four separate days; this suited me because some of them were quite long and tiring. I found the declaration after each one to be very important. It was good to say aloud those words that were to enable me to build on my faith and to resist the devil.

For me it has been a gradual change. I am now more confident about my abilities and myself. God has really changed my life around – and I now know there is more to come. He has blessed me so much. I feel closer to Him now and I know He will keep His promise to be with me no matter what I go through. I still have my bad days but I am able to cope with everything much better now.

I am now working again, and helping with Sunday school, and I have progressed so much during the past year. I think that without Freedom in Christ I would not have been able to achieve so much in so short a time. It is so important to know who you are in Christ, and to spend time getting to know Jesus and reading His word. Now I just want to encourage people who may be going through the same things. There *is* hope – I am living proof of that. Nothing is impossible with God.

Not every thought is your own

"Could I have been listening to Satan all this time, thinking it was God?" In my experience, the answer to that question is an emphatic "yes". We are told that Satan disguises himself as an angel of light. Look at what Paul says on the matter:

> The Spirit clearly says that in later times some will abandon the faith and follow deceiving spirits and things taught by demons. (1 Timothy 4:1)

Satan often takes advantage of those who are desperate to hear God speaking to them. To start with, the voice they hear recommends apparently good things, but over time it becomes more and more bizarre and, if they keep listening, usually leads to their life falling apart in some way.

Both Peter and Suzanne struggled with bizarre thoughts. Peter believed that the thoughts were his own and that he must, therefore, be weird, whereas Suzanne thought she had a hotline to God. Both were deceived. The Bible is quite clear that Satan can put thoughts into our minds. It's a great relief to many to discover that the intrusive or bizarre thoughts they are experiencing are not their own.

Usually these thoughts subside once someone goes through The Steps. However, Christians need to be continually aware that the enemy can put tempting, accusing or deceptive thoughts into our minds and get into the habit of "taking every thought captive":

> We demolish arguments and every pretension that sets itself up against the knowledge of God, and we take captive every thought to make it obedient to Christ. (2 Corinthians 10:5)

Some get hung up on asking, "Is that thought from the enemy?" That's the wrong question. The issue is not so much where the thought is coming from but whether or not it is true. We need to get into the habit of holding up every thought to the light of God's word and, if it turns out not to be true, simply discarding it.

Christians and demons

We've talked about Satan having footholds in our lives and looked at the fact that deceiving spirits will try to get us to believe lies. That raises a question about the relationship between Christians and demons.

It's very important to stress that I am not talking about Christians being "possessed" by demons in the sense that they could be completely taken over or taken back by demons. You have been purchased by the blood of the Lamb (1 Peter 1:18–19). At the centre of your being, your spirit is connected to God's Spirit and Satan can't have you back. In other words, this is not about ownership (or "possession"). I am simply talking about degrees of influence that the enemy can gain in your life to disrupt your walk with the Lord or even to try to get you to further his own agenda.

Of the three things that we're up against in our Christian walk – the world, the flesh and the devil – the good news is that this area of the devil is the most easily resolvable of the three. Jesus came to destroy the devil's work (1 John 3:8) and in Christ we have the right to take back any ground we have given him in our lives. The Steps to Freedom in Christ is simply a structured way to do that, but it's only effective in so far as you are genuinely prepared to repent and then do some work to stand in the freedom you will gain.

Suggestions for further reading

- *Finding God's Will in Spiritually Deceptive Times* (Anderson, Harvest House, 2003)
- *Battle Plan for Spiritual Warfare* (Wasmond & Miller, Harvest House, 2004).

Available from your local Christian bookshop or directly from Freedom in Christ Ministries.

Chapter 5

Renewing our minds

Taking hold of our freedom is the key to moving on as a growing disciple. However, it's one thing getting free but quite another staying free.

Let's look at how we can go on to stand in the freedom gained during The Steps appointment.

Jenny's story

"When I practised my New Age meditations I would see my husband in a coffin, and was full of terror..."

I was born out of wedlock 54 years ago. At that time there was a great stigma attached to this, and I was referred to as my mother's "bastard". I grew up apologising for having been born. The insecurity and emotional pain I suffered from would often make me physically sick, especially if I went to a friend's house for the weekend.

Mum worked long hours and spent her weekends away with her various boyfriends, and I was often left with my grandma or a neighbour. Mum and Grandma were Spiritualists, and brought me up to believe that everyone went to heaven. I don't think there was a Bible in the house but at the age of eight I made an altar to Jesus in my bedroom. I made a cross to go on it and prayed there in a childlike way but I did not hear the Gospel until I was 21. At that time I thought Christians were soft and spineless people. I scoffed at them, convinced that I was right in my judgments.

When I was still in my teens Mum encouraged me to use the Ouija board, and I remember doing this again at college and thinking I had a special gift of contacting departed spirits. On the outside I looked fine, but inside I was crippled with anxiety, bordering on fear in the company of men. As I grew up I could not eat or drink in the presence of a man. I saw different psychiatrists and psychologists and began taking tranquillisers at the age of 16 – being told to make them part of my diet!

This dependence lasted till I was about 38. Because of the grounding in Spiritualism, I progressed into New Age faith. I studied to be a medium and spiritual healer, completing all my training with SAGB (The Spiritualist Association of Great Britain). My mother encouraged me by saying that my great-grandmother had been an excellent medium, so I decided to follow in her footsteps and put my heart and soul into it. Imagine my shock when I met Jesus many years later and understood how badly I had been deceived – and had deceived myself!

I did not of course know how I was opening up to evil. I just felt that life was always against me and that I must have a difficult and heavy load or "karma" to work through. I went into past-life therapy and saw myself as Judas betraying our Lord, and I cried for several days. The New Age teaching embraces Jesus but in a counterfeit way, because there is no mention of the cross. Satan weaves a very similar picture of the kingdom of heaven except that it is actually a total blasphemy of all that is right and true. For there is no mention of sin and consequently no room for the need of salvation. Jesus' sacrifice for sin is denied, as the atonement had no place in their teaching.

Throughout all this, God in His infinite mercy and tender

compassion was intent on drawing me to Himself. I see now that through all my difficult experiences He was bringing people across my path to lead me into truth. I heard the Gospel but just could not understand it. It is certainly true that Satan blinds the minds of believers and "that the Gospel is veiled to those who are perishing" (2 Corinthians 4:3).

I ended up in a Sai Baba cult and at this time I started thinking I must be gay. I clearly remember something entering my body and from then on I started feeling attracted to women. Thank God I never entered into a sexual relationship with a woman. Sai Baba has since been exposed as an un-holy man, but sad to say he still has followers.

At the age of 45 I met and married a man who was a chronic alcoholic and had already lost two wives because of it. I felt at complete rock bottom and trapped in a disastrous relationship with nowhere to run to. I had moved two hundred miles to be with him. I was like a moth being drawn to a candle flame. I now know that this move was Satan's trump card, and he thought I would soon be crushed by these events. When I practised my New Age meditations I would see my husband in a coffin, and was full of terror and distress.

But God in His sovereign wisdom saw that I was now ripe for salvation. I had completely come to the end of myself. One day I simply collapsed in a soggy heap and cried out for help. From a desperate heart, "in my anguish I cried to the Lord. And He answered by setting me free" (Psalm 118:5)... BUT – I cried to all the holy men I could think of! Buddha, Mohammed, Allah and Jesus – probably in that order. Yet I felt a warm, comforting presence filling my soul and I heard the word "Repent". The events following were God Himself working out my future.

I was led to a Pentecostal church but I still did not know what was happening to me. Jesus was carrying me – stepping out with me through all the tangled undergrowth of my past life. And I was holding on for dear life! Looking back, I see what a hazardous journey it was that we took together, but my Jesus was in control. He would never let me go.

The pastor gave me a book called *Living Free in Christ* by Neil Anderson, and after reading only two pages I received the revelation that would change me for ever. The Lord showed me His feet being nailed to the cross and then He let me see the evil that had oppressed me. I was thrown down onto the bed and began writhing and crying, out of control. It lasted for a few minutes and when I went into the bathroom to wash my face I saw, looking back at me in the mirror, the figure of a monk. He was short and fat in stature and he was laughing at me. I was terrified. What was happening to me?

The pastor – perhaps understandably – did not really want to get involved at this point. But I was beside myself with desperation for help. But what should I do? I wore a cross and chain around my neck at all times, but it kept coming off at night. I would find it in knots at the bottom of the bed. Then objects began to fly off shelves and all the electrics in the house went berserk...

I have since vowed that I will never see anyone left this way if the Lord allows me to help others. I wrote to Neil Anderson in America and the UK office of Freedom in Christ Ministries put me in touch with a church in Sussex. I made the necessary journey and was taken under the wing of some loving, caring people who arranged for me to be led through The Steps to Freedom. What an experience that was – one that I shall never forget.

It was during a coffee break that a really significant thing happened. I heard an inner voice declare: "I won't come out unless there is a man here!" I knew I was at the heart of a spiritual battle centred in that moment on my basic fear of men. But, glory to His name, the demons did come out, and after the very last Step I ended up completely free.

However, this was to be just the start of a real and often frustrating battle to actually walk in this freedom – the freedom purchased for me on the cross at Calvary. I was still a baby Christian and had no idea about putting on the armour or how to stand and resist. True freedom has been a gradual process and The Steps to Freedom together with Neil's books have been a priceless part of that journey.

Lasting progress had come with strong foundations in the word of God. He encouraged me to put everything aside to concentrate on building my Temple. I gave up my design business and soaked myself in the Scriptures. I saw how important it is to seek His kingdom and His righteousness first, in order that everything else should fall into place. God carried me through the dark days of my husband's drinking and violent bouts. At these times Jesus would always be very close and impart to me a verse of Scripture to strengthen and comfort me.

He also showed me how to pray for Ron and how to pray the word back to God on my husband's behalf. Satan craftily comes to steal away any God-given blessings, so my Lord has encouraged me to practise the disciplines of memorising and meditating on the word, fasting and seeking Him diligently through prayer. By His grace He has allowed me to make spiritual progress and I rejoice at the radical changes I have seen taking place in my husband. He has now come out of denial concerning his drinking and he has received Jesus as his Lord and Saviour. We now pray together and read the Scriptures every day.

What is more, the Lord has healed me emotionally so that I now have His peace in many of the previously troubled areas of my life. We are still working on the sexual side, but we are learning patience. In our walk of faith we need to trust God completely to do His own work in His own time, believing that complete deliverance is waiting for us a little further down the path.

Often it seems that God heals things we think are not so important, building up to the breakthrough we need. And as He can see the picture from start to finish we must bow to His wisdom and sovereignty. He has a plan and we can rest in that knowledge. Ron doesn't get as angry so often now and he no longer suffers the physical consequences of his drinking.

The most wonderful gift God has given me is a complete healing of my relationship with my mother. I have stood in the gap for her and she has come to a saving knowledge of Christ after 80 years of being in the wilderness of Spiritualism. I have had the privilege of seeing her delivered and planted in a church where she is pastored. Both she and my stepfather go to worship together and he is 88 years old! God's grace is truly amazing. All He asks of us is that we believe and trust Him and obey His word.

The Lord has been so close to me when Ron was in drink. Each time He has given me a scripture to hold on to and to quote at Satan. Sometimes if I have not put my armour on I have had to pay the penalty of getting wounded. But my heavenly Father has tenderly picked me up and set my feet on the path again. I am constantly being reminded from Ephesians 6:12 that "we wrestle not against flesh and blood, but against principalities and powers..." Our Christian life is a training ground on which God makes our feet "like hinds' feet", and our arms strong enough to "bend a bow of bronze"...

Two years ago a door opened for me to teach and preach God's word in a church that had got so run down that only four people met there. There are now 16 and it is growing steadily. I have a wonderful pastor who takes a genuine interest in me, and I stand on the promises of God and know that with His help my marriage will be a wonderful picture of Christ's relationship with His church.

I can only keep giving God the glory for the great things He has done in my life already, and for the divine grace and mercy which brought me out of darkness into His marvellous light. Like Joseph we can say, "What was intended to harm us, God meant for our good" (Genesis 50:20).

Having "closed the doors" to the enemy was not the end of the story. Jenny helpfully emphasises the need for an ongoing commitment to believe the truth in God's word. Once we have repented of anything that gives the enemy the ability to influence our thinking, the next step is simply faith – in other words we have to believe the truth and commit ourselves to it.

Jenny talks about the armour of God (see Ephesians 6:10–20). Note that the first piece of armour Paul mentions in this picture of a Roman soldier's protection is the belt of truth. It was this belt that held everything else together. Truth is fundamental to walking in freedom and we need to put on the belt of truth and the other pieces of the armour of God every day. That does not mean, of course, simply "saying the right words" – we put on the belt of truth when we commit ourselves to believing that what God says is true and acting on it. We ensure that the breastplate of righteousness is in place when we recognise the truth that, despite the accusing, condemning insinuations of the enemy, we are righteous because of who we are in Christ.

Strongholds

This commitment to truth is easier said than done, however, because of unhelpful thought patterns we have developed, which are difficult to break. These are "strongholds", mental habit patterns burned into our minds over time or by the trauma of certain experiences. Some call them flesh patterns. They represent the old nature, how we have learned to live our lives independently of God.

As we were growing up we did not have the presence of God in our lives, nor the knowledge of His ways. During the early years of our lives we learned to live independently of God – He did not figure in our thinking. We really had no choice.

For example, I learned early on in life that when I felt low, a packet of biscuits (yes, a whole packet!) made me feel better. Eventually it became a coping mechanism and now, whenever I have a bad day, that thought pattern kicks in and I am tempted to overeat. There is nothing wrong with eating or food – but using it as a means to meet a need like that is acting independently of God. He is the God of all comfort and more than ready to pour it into my life.

When we became Christians nobody pushed a "clear" button in our minds. All the false beliefs and coping mechanisms we had developed were still there. Sometimes strongholds show themselves in things we feel we should do but don't seem able to, or things we know we shouldn't do and don't feel able to stop. The truth, however, is that God loves us. He would never ask us to do something that we couldn't do. He never asks us to jump over a barrier and then puts it so high that we can't do it. He loves us too much to do anything like that. So, if that's how it feels, we're talking about strongholds getting in the way.

If we don't know how to tear down these mental strongholds we may well give up and conclude (wrongly), "That's just the way I am – I can't change." "I occasionally have fits of anger: well that's just me." Or "I'm just very shy – I can't change." Other examples of strongholds would include feelings of inferiority, insecurity and inadequacy.

You may recall that Rachel, in the first story we looked at, talked about how she was taught this strategy and that it was her key to remaining free. I remember saying to her after her freedom appointment that she seemed to have believed the lie that she was dirty. She surprised me with the vehemence of her response: "No, that's not right at all!".

"Oh," I said, "it's just that you seem to have mentioned feeling dirty a lot."

"Well," she said, "I *am* dirty. It's not a lie!"

Past experiences had taught Rachel to see herself and her body as dirty. I suspect that her subsequent anorexia, self-harm and addictions were simply ways she used to try to cope with – i.e. blot out – those negative feelings.

The key to her ongoing freedom was to know what is really true: that through Christ she has been made pure, spotless and perfectly clean; that God welcomes her into His presence and is proud of her as His growing child. For Rachel the lie was deeply ingrained. She had taken the lie that she was dirty as fact for so long that she had to make an effort to start to believe what was really true. Yet, once she had closed the doors to the enemy's influence in her life, she was able to do that.

How are Christians transformed? Paul says clearly that it's through renewing our minds (Romans 12:2). It's as we commit ourselves wholeheartedly to believing what is true and throwing out old ways of thinking that we are changed to become more like Jesus.

Katy too was helped by learning to break strongholds.

Katy's story

"At boarding school there was a large emphasis on appearance: a girl with a scholarship, coke-bottle-bottom glasses and boys' jeans was bound for trouble..."

I was the fourth child in a large family. We had an idyllic childhood, living on a sizeable farm and holidaying by the sea every year. In reception class, when I was asked what my mother did, I said, "She stays at home!"

"What does your father do?"

"He stays at home too!"

An anxious look from the teacher – it was a state school in a deprived area...

"He must do something," she said, racking her brains to think what her knowledge of our family was. "Where do you live?"

"On a farm," I said.

"Then your father's a farmer!" she said, clearly relieved.

As far as I was concerned, my father was around the whole time, in and out of the house, and we had lovely long holidays after harvest.

Job? What job?

When I started going to school and (coincidentally) got glasses, I began to discover that life wasn't that golden. I got teased a lot for my glasses, which thickened rapidly with each six-month check. I found that things seemed to change at home too. My appearance wasn't so enchanting any more. And when I did jobs around the home, nothing I did seemed good enough. The car wasn't washed properly. I didn't polish my shoes well enough. I got the general feeling of not quite coming up to scratch. And things got worse as I got older.

At secondary (boarding) school, there was a large emphasis on appearance. A girl with a scholarship, coke-bottle-bottom glasses and boys' jeans was bound for trouble. I got quite a bit of flak, which ground me down. My way of reacting was to wear jeans, jumpers and flip-flops all year round, even in the snow: I thought I was above their opinions, but in reality I was too scared to compete, because I just knew I would be found wanting.

My self-esteem plummeted during this time and things changed at home too. The bumper harvest of my early childhood gave way to more troubled times and my father took to studying in his office for long hours. His relationship with my mother became strained. I hardly ever saw him. They were critical of each other, and of us children. They would point out things they saw as faults and would not praise you to your face for the things you thought you had done well. We would all hear praise for our siblings, however, and great sibling rivalry began to develop. Our home life seemed to become a breeding ground for it.

I had great support at boarding school from two elder

sisters, though. And this helped to protect me from deeper isolation and verbal bullying. I buried myself in work, in the world of books, and started reading large numbers of romantic novels – sometimes three a day. My sense of identity blurred: there was pressure to see oneself as a family member rather than as an individual – the strength of the family was underlined. And my own self-esteem sank lower.

Boys? What boys? I came into contact with very few, being at a girls' boarding school. I was rejected by those I saw because of my appearance. I put on weight and started to comfort-eat. Again my strategy was not to compete, so as not to get rejected.

When I got contact lenses at the age of 17 things began to change. Suddenly, quite a few boys started talking to me who hadn't ever done so before. I couldn't handle the attention really. I didn't know how to say no. I was so desperate to be accepted and so scared of rejection that I ended up having several sexual experiences I didn't want to have, simply because I couldn't speak up for myself. To be honest I don't think I really knew what I wanted. One part of my heart was fine with the concept of sex before marriage – I wasn't religious – but another part of it was screaming, and I felt really abused by these encounters, however fleeting and non-penetrative they were.

I became anxious and depressed, and again reacted by vowing not to compete. I "gave up men". However, these encounters still went on. I could identify with women who had been raped, because that is exactly how I felt. I closed up; my family knew I'd changed and become moody again, but didn't try to find out why.

During this time I started wondering what life was all about. At boarding school I had my first contact with organised Christianity. I listened. I did some deep thinking. I figured that it should all be true – all the bits of the puzzle seemed to be there... I asked Jesus into my life when I was twelve or thirteen. However, it just didn't seem to happen for me. There was no flood of faith. No confidence. No change whatsoever. In fact I became more and more worried about doing the right thing, and more and more self-critical. I could see now why I didn't measure up. I gave up. In this, too, I had failed. My spiritual inclinations fell dormant for a couple of years – to be reawakened by a visiting American girl called Jo, who introduced me to Shirley McLaine and the whole New Age scene.

I read avidly; I talked – *we* talked! I now had one important thing that was missing from the Christianity lark – someone to discuss stuff with. Jo and I would talk about "spiritual" matters deep into the night. When she went back to the States we wrote to one another. At my new school there was a chap who was into it all too. I got books on developing your psychic powers, and tried astral projection, ghost writing, auras, etc. My friends in the Christian forum were very worried about me and used to tell me they were praying for me. I actually pooh-poohed them. This new teaching was much more "spiritual" than the legalism I had observed their Christianity to be.

However, as I searched, I could see that everything pointed towards the idea of God being within yourself: no, to *you being God*. Reality is what you perceive as creator, they said. I knew this wasn't right. I was getting more and more screwed up in myself. I knew I didn't have the answers. In all the writings – New Age, Buddhism, Hare Krishna, Hindu – Jesus was portrayed as pure white light. And I became more and more attracted to this essential purity. It was what I longed for. The school had a mission, and at last I saw someone who knew what he was talking about. He had first-hand knowledge. He had a relationship with this Jesus.

I knew that this was what I wanted. As I listened to him going through the Lord's Prayer line by line, explaining the

Gospel, it all made sense. Suddenly, I knew that Jesus was in the room with me.

"What took you so long?" asked my Saviour, in the most gentle and fun-loving way.

I was changed: a new creation. I was full of joy and new confidence on the inside. I was also ragged mercilessly by my family and was very isolated for the first year of my faith. But when I went to university to study medicine I slowly plugged into a church and a home group for the support I needed.

In spite of my new-found joy, I still struggled with a high level of anxiety and low self-esteem. I avoided romantic contact and drank heavily in the relative safety of the student bar. As my studies falteringly progressed – I failed more exams than I passed, but eventually got passes in them all – I seemed to get worse. I found the hospital environment exceedingly stressful. You were judged on everything you did or knew. My first consultant was sleeping with one of his juniors, and eyeing up another. And he had a blistering tongue. We were 19 to 20 years old. On the surface I performed, but internally I was not coping very well. I was scared and low. I didn't believe in myself. I tried to talk to people about the way I felt but they couldn't help. I felt totally alone, abandoned by family and friends.

During this dark time, God showed me that He was still there, that He would keep me going if I would just put my trust in Him. Soon after this I met George. He was a Christian who had recently joined my university. I became convinced God was telling me that this was the man for me. I was terrified, and rather relieved when he started going out with someone else. We were both sent on a placement to another hospital the day after that relationship ended, and we talked. We shared meals and talked just about every evening. I found myself being open, being accepted, and for the first time I felt that someone really accepted me. We started going out a couple of months later. I grew spiritually as well as personally. George counselled me. He listened. *He cared*. I felt accepted. We got married within a couple of years.

I failed finals, but passed the resit. We both worked very hard and rarely saw each other or our families, because we were junior doctors. We tried hard at church, too. But when was trying hard good enough for God? I felt as if I was struggling up a sheer cliff face. I was very critical of my husband; I was critical of myself. I had been a Christian for ten years when we met someone who had such confidence in his faith and in God that we were inspired, and went to visit him. For the first time we were given teaching about "Who you are in Christ"... and our lives were transformed. The initial joy I had had when I was converted came back to me. I started to base my confidence on who God said I was, rather than on my own performance.

However, I still struggled with guilt about my sexual experiences, my low self-esteem, my critical spirit... My sister-in-law gave me *Victory over the Darkness* by Neil Anderson to read. Here was the teaching on "Who I am in Christ" – in print! I started to read. I went on to read *The Bondage Breaker* by Neil Anderson and identified with many of the stories in it. Here was an answer to my struggles. A direct approach to my internal conflicts. I went through The Steps to Freedom on my own, which helped enormously.

I was knocked for six when I had my first baby. Suddenly I was fearful again, and exquisitely sensitive to everything anyone said. I saw lots of comments as criticisms when they weren't meant to be. I went to a church and did the Steps again with a wonderful pair of women who gave up their Saturday to be with me. We went through all the themes again. There was a greater power in confessing and renouncing with others (James 5:16). I came out feeling peaceful, knowing that my past was resolved and now left behind –

where it belonged. My responsibility now was to take hold of today and to renew my mind.

That was three years ago. I have changed and am changing still. My discernment and prophetic gifting, which had been twisted into criticism, is now being practised to build up others. I am able to live in the tension of shades of grey rather than having the need to paint everything either black or white. Several people have said they are no longer scared of me! I have less drive to control what happens in my work and family life now that I accept myself for what I am. I still fight the habit of trying to do everything in my own strength, but I am practising relying on God – and I have opened myself up to accountability with others. I think that has been a key thing in my walk – not to do it alone. Doing The Steps with others sealed my freedom in Christ. Working on breaking strongholds with a couple of trusted friends holding me accountable has helped far more than trying to do it all on my own.

Stronghold-busting

Katy continued to walk in the freedom that she won during the Steps process because she did some work on breaking strongholds. To illustrate further how a stronghold works in our minds, imagine that you are a farmer and you drive your Land Rover across a wet field. It will create some ruts. If you do that every day for some time, you won't even have to steer after a while. The Land Rover will simply follow the ruts. In fact, any attempt to steer out of the ruts will be met with resistance. That's how a stronghold works. If we don't think too hard, our minds will just fall into the same old comfortable thought patterns.

But you can steer out of the ruts of habitual faulty thinking by making a sustained effort over a period of time. If you've learned something wrongly, you can relearn it. If you have programmed your computer badly, you can reprogram it. But you have to want to. You have to choose to. I have a strategy for this, which I call "Stronghold-busting".

Stronghold-busting is a way of renewing your mind that requires you to grit your teeth and make a decision to believe what God says is true and go on believing it for a six-week period despite what your feelings (based on your past experiences) tell you.

First of all, you need to determine the lie you have been believing (any way you are thinking that is not in line with what God says about you in the Bible). You will become aware of what these are as you go through the Steps process. The key thing is to ignore what you feel but commit yourself wholeheartedly to God's truth.

Then, find as many Bible verses as you can that state the truth and write them down. Write a prayer or declaration based on the formula: "I renounce the lie that... I announce the truth that..." For example: "I renounce the lie that I am dirty because of my past sexual experiences. I joyfully announce the truth that I am clean and holy, that my heart has been sprinkled by the blood of Jesus to cleanse me from a guilty conscience and that I can come confidently into God's presence any time I like. There is no condemnation for those who, like me, are in Christ Jesus. Thank you, Lord, that you look at me and smile! Amen."

Finally, read the Bible verses and say the prayer/declaration every day for 40 days, all the time reminding yourself that God is truth and that if He has said it, it really is true for you. Don't worry if you miss a day or two (this is not a legalistic ritual), but do persevere until you have completed a total of 40 days. In fact you may wish to go on longer, and you will almost certainly want to come back and do it again at some point in the future.

Why 40 days? Psychologists will tell you that it takes about six weeks to form or break a habit and, once any spiritual issue has been dealt with, a stronghold is simply a habitual way of thinking. If it's a particularly ingrained way of thinking, you may well want to do more than 40 days or come back and revisit it in the future, but please do not stop before the 40 days are up.

Ed Silvoso tells of how a pastor friend of his watched a concrete wall being demolished. It withstood ten, then fifteen, then 30, then 35 blows with no visible sign of being weakened. That's how it can feel as you work through a stronghold-buster day after day. However, each day you renounce the lie and commit yourself to truth is making a difference. A wall might appear not to have been weakened right up to, say, 37 swings of a demolition ball. However, sooner or later (say on the 38th swing), a few small cracks will appear. On the next these cracks will get bigger, and so on until, finally, the wall completely collapses. Even though only the final three swings appear to have had an effect, without the previous 37 the wall would not have fallen.

The whole point of a stronghold is that it feels true. That means that for most of the 40 days the stronghold-busting exercise will *feel* like a waste of time. It's crucial to hang on in there and get through it. Every day the crucial question you face is this: are you going to believe what God says is true about you in His word, or are you going to believe what your past experiences have taught you?

Remember that it takes time to demolish a stronghold and get rid of negative thinking. Just because the thoughts recur doesn't mean it's not working – it's whether or not you choose to believe the thoughts that is important. It requires a concerted effort over time, but you can have every expectation that your mind will become pure and those thoughts will eventually fade.

There is an example of a completed stronghold-buster I did to help me with my weakness for comfort-eating in chapter 10.

Suggestions for further reading

- *Freedom from Fear* (Anderson & Miller, Monarch, 2003)
- *Getting Anger Under Control* (Anderson & Miller, Harvest House, 2002)

Available from your local Christian bookshop or directly from Freedom in Christ Ministries.

Chapter 6

Freedom from depression

Depression and anxiety are the major mental-health issues facing the Western world. In the UK, stress, anxiety and depression affect up to one in four people at any one time: over 1,000,000 people are dependent on tranquillisers and more than 5,000 people take their own lives each year; there are 19,000 suicide attempts by adolescents alone.

One leading expert forecasts that by 2020 severe depression will be the second leading cause of death after heart disease.

In Marie's story, you will see clearly how, in her case, doors left open to the enemy had a devastating and debilitating effect on someone who simply wanted to do her best to serve God. When she dealt with them through repentance and believing the truth, it was the start of a lasting and decisive change.

Marie's story

"My mother was by this time practising as a medium herself, and wasn't beyond casting spells on people against whom she had grievances..."

My earliest memory as a child is being told I was unwanted. I never questioned it because I had nothing to compare with it. That was just how it was, but the sense of rejection and failure those words carried became rooted in my soul.

Our "normal" church was the "Christian" Spiritualist Church. I had no choice about attending, as my mother and grandmother took me along with them. Although I had little or no true Christian experience, I always had a sense that what was happening was spiritually wrong. I remember feeling scared stiff when the elderly medium would go into a trance and begin to speak as a little girl or a grown man. I was even more scared when one night a "message" came through for me – a message that appeared to come from my half-sister's dead father. The words that were spoken revealed a secret that only he and I knew about. As a Christian adult, I now recognise the deception that was at work. But if the enemy was trying to prove himself real to me, it actually had completely the opposite effect. Because, at the tender age of eleven, I began an earnest quest to find God for myself.

I wanted to go to a "real" church and went along with my cousins to the local Catholic church. I was learning Latin at school and became completely entranced by the mystery of their rituals, ancient language and smells. At the age of twelve I asked my parents if I could become a Catholic and, as they raised no objection, I began to make preparations.

Then at New Year 1973 God suddenly broke into my life. I was on holiday with my sister, who was already a committed Christian. She took me to a Bible study on John chapter 3, where I heard the gospel presented in a manner I could understand. I felt the conviction of the Holy Spirit calling me as He called Nicodemus to be born again. So on New Year's Eve I gave my life over to Jesus.

Back home again I carried on attending the Catholic church, but something inside me had changed. I found myself reaching out for something beyond the beauty of the rituals and language: I wanted Jesus. So I went to a Christian teacher at school and asked him whether we could form a Christian union. He agreed, and through that group I began to grow and develop in my faith. I played the piano for the young people's group at the local Baptist church. I didn't know what a Baptist church was but it felt right to go, so I did. I then joined a church Bible study group and soon afterwards was baptised as a believer.

I realise now that, while I had a great social life at the church with Christian young people of my own age, I didn't really learn much more about being a Christian, what difference it should have made to the way I lived, or what difficulties I might meet along the way. I was unaware that I was engaged in a winnable spiritual battle with an enemy whose power I had already seen and who I believed was equally as powerful as God. In many ways I was set up to fail.

My relationship with my mother deteriorated. She was by this time practising as a medium herself, and wasn't beyond casting spells on people against whom she had grievances. It wasn't at all easy being the only born-again baptised believer in a house dedicated to the occult. My life was totally controlled by my mother. I was not allowed to choose my friends, and I certainly was not allowed to move out and get a flat of my own. I envied the freedom of other young people and eventually became desperate to escape. This I did by marrying one of the boys from the Christian youth group.

We moved away to where he was a schoolteacher and where he also pastored a small Baptist church on a part-time basis. So, at the tender age of 20, I found myself catapulted into what I now see as a totally ridiculous situation, as I became a pastor's wife living in a manse. I had entered into marriage to escape a difficult home environment, without thinking through the consequences. The result was that I found myself not only joined with a husband I didn't really love or want but also doing a part-time job that came with no set job description, but many, many expectations. And basically I failed – big time.

My husband was a good friend, but I never wanted him to be a lover, as I didn't really love him. Consequently, our wedding night was an utter disaster, and the relationship was doomed to failure from that moment on. Very quickly we began sleeping in separate bedrooms, as I couldn't bear him to touch me.

In addition, he had been brought up in an environment where his godly and submissive mother had devoted herself to meeting his and his siblings' every need, so it soon became plain that, on top of working full-time for the extra money it brought in, I was expected to bake bread, cakes and pastries, sew and mend, keep the house meticulously clean and tidy, entertain and throw dinner parties where everything must be homemade, and, in my spare time (!), conquer a garden that hadn't been touched for years. On top of all this came the expectations of the church, to which I was a constant disappointment, because I would often forget to do the flowers for Sunday until late on Saturday evening when the shops were shut, or fail to take time off to chair the Women's Meetings or scout round the village drumming up support to fill the Sunday school with children.

After three years of this life, it began to feel like a loveless trap. I became depressed and started to dream of waking up somewhere else one day. It was like a voice screaming in my head, pleading to be allowed to be myself instead of the person everyone expected me to be – which wasn't really me at all. I talked about my situation at work, and with the full approval of my manager (which mattered a lot in those days!) moved out into a rented room in the house of one of my workmates' mother.

And so it became official. I had failed. I'd failed my husband, the church, our friends, our parents and, above all, God. One "friend" wrote me a letter telling me how God hated divorce, and that if I went ahead with this separation then there would be no way back for me. This of course was a lie, but I believed it. So for the next four years I turned my back on God and tried to live my life without Him.

When I left my husband, all my Christian "friends" deserted me like rats abandoning a sinking ship, with one exception – Tim. He was single, almost 40, and still living at home with his parents, and through observing their often difficult marriage, and ours as well, he had come to realise that not everything is black and white. There are shades of grey, and some marriages – even Christian ones – can be abusive. He understood, and remained my only Christian friend. We started "going out" as companions together and eventually fell in love. I see this as the grace of God, because I think that without Tim's love and friendship supporting me I would have crashed completely through what lay ahead.

In 1985 I moved out of my digs and bought a house of my own. It was completely run-down (and therefore cheap!), and the renovation project acted as a substitution in my life for the big hole left by cutting out church. I loved my independence and threw myself wholeheartedly into my career. I quickly rose to become Manager's Assistant, as I made it clear to my bosses that I belonged 100% to the bank.

This had its drawbacks, such as being on 24-hour call for the alarm system, which meant night call-outs to a branch twelve miles away. I hated returning to an empty house in the dark and began to be filled with the fear of being attacked. My fear turned into reality one night when a gang of youths followed me home. I was too afraid to get out of the car and walk to my door, so drove to a work colleague's house. Her husband called the police.

The next morning I wrote my car off. Then I quickly spiralled downwards into depression and was put on medication. But even with sleeping tablets I was too afraid to sleep. I would barricade myself into my bedroom and stay awake all night reading. I would then be too exhausted to do anything during the day. My career folded as I went on long-term sick leave. In fact I only ever returned part-time. During the nine months that followed Tim and I became engaged, and we married in 1987. Many of my fears were put to one side as we shared our life together, but I was still very fragile mentally.

At the end of 1987 we sold my house and returned to Tim's family home to live with his elderly mother. We set about modernising it and building a modern annexe for her adjoining the main cottage, which she would share with her brother and sister.

This was the period in which our children, Mark and Ian, were born. We were very happy and settled and all seemed right with our world. Except that as a Christian couple we had been leaving God out of our relationship. Tim had always gone to chapel. He couldn't avoid it, as the chapel was in our garden! It had been built by the family and maintained by the family, and was eventually to be closed by the family. But Tim had never been able to persuade me to go; I just didn't want to get involved.

The crunch came with the birth of our children. I felt the stirrings of my dormant faith when I sensed God placing a challenge before us – either to bring these children up in the Christian faith or to forget it for ever. Now the chapel in the garden wasn't the place to bring up a young family. In fact, everyone who attended the chapel either lived in our house or was related. This led to the interesting situation in which we could be having Sunday lunch together in the house, wash up and walk out of the back door and into the chapel, and suddenly be holding a service together. It wasn't really fellowship, but it was definitely family!

And unfortunately there was an element of control again. If we ever wanted a Sunday off we had to face the "Spanish Inquisition" and give reasons to excuse ourselves as the numbers game was played. Attendance at the service was paramount, and failure to be there brought not only a heavy sense of guilt, but definite bad vibrations – which we had to live with in the house as well, of course!

Tim and I felt that if we made the decision to bring our children up in the faith, then it would mean leaving the family chapel and joining a larger church. We needed to be with other young families. But this would inevitably raise a question mark over the viability of the chapel. This obviously placed a great burden of responsibility upon us, as well as a heavy sense of guilt at letting the generations down.

But it had to be done, and early in 1990 we joined the local Baptist church in a much larger town nearby. It was only when we began attending a "lively" church that we both realised how spiritually hungry we had become for the word of God. The first year when Tim joined the church's rolling discipleship programme there was such a change in him that in the second year I signed up too. Through this course we both recognised that God was calling us into whole-time Christian ministry. I clearly remember the moment when I knelt before God and gave my life back to Him unreservedly. I deliberately laid my life on the altar before Him and gave Him permission to work in my life, doing whatever He needed to do to make me the person He needed me to be to fulfil my destiny. It was easily prayed, but I didn't reckon on how God might take me literally. What happened to me next is best described as a "dark night of the soul".

Having handed my life over to the Lord to do with me as He saw fit, I was suddenly plunged into a pit of the blackest depression. I had suffered an attack of depression twice already, but this third attack within five years was by far the worst. I spiralled downhill rapidly, barely able to walk unaided, unable to stand the daylight, and confined largely to my bed. I was eventually diagnosed as suffering from ME, and became incapable of looking after my small children. Once again I felt a complete failure. I was so ill and desperate to be well that I began to investigate New Age medicines. I tried every type of therapy and bought every type of medicine I could lay my hands on. I was completely hooked, but failed to see that the "healing" they brought was only ever temporary, leaving me in the end feeling worse than before.

It was in this way that I dug myself deeper and deeper into the pit of deception and despair. I had repeated nightmares, which always involved watching my own funeral. I began to speculate that perhaps everyone would be better off without me. I battled with this sense of wanting to die for 18 months, but although I used to plan how it might be done, I was always too much of a coward to follow it through. This pit of despair was such a contrast to the spiritual euphoria of just a couple of months earlier.

However, God knew what He was doing, and I have since learned that there is only one way to get to the Promised Land, and that is by travelling through the wilderness. Because it is there that God can really work on us, removing the dross of Egypt and shaping us for what lies ahead. I clearly remember one Sunday when I had to be helped on two arms into church and just sat feeling very alone and isolated while the service went on as usual around me. There were close on 400 people in the sanctuary that morning but as far as I was concerned I might have been the only one present. For God spoke to me quite clearly.

Our minister was preaching on Psalm 51: "Create in me a pure heart, O God, and renew a steadfast spirit within me." I hadn't prayed in 18 months but that morning I prayed in the words of that psalm, and God heard and answered my prayer. At the end of the service a couple came up to me and asked if they might pray for my healing. I remember being horrified at the thought. Even worse, they wanted to bring a "healer" with them! However, by this time my feelings of low esteem were so bad that I felt trapped anyway and just resigned myself to "putting up" with this forthcoming "ministry". A date was set and the evening duly arrived. The "healer", who at that time had an international healing ministry within the Baptist denomination, encouraged me in working through something like Step 7 of The Steps to Freedom in Christ, which deals with generational sin and inherited characteristics. The Holy Spirit had caused him to discern my occult heritage.

As he prayed, I experienced an enormous weight pressing down on my head – a weight so heavy that it almost knocked me over. As the healer went out of the door, he left me with a scripture, Psalm 107:43: "Whoever is wise, let him... consider the great love of the Lord."

When I awoke the next morning the fog in my mind had cleared enough for me to begin to read God's word again, and God had given me a hunger and thirst to do so. As I lay in bed, I began to meditate on "the great love of the Lord". And, through reading *Victory over the Darkness* and *The Bondage Breaker* by Neil Anderson, I came to realise just how much God really did love me. I understood the truth that my identity was in being an accepted, secure and significant child of God, instead of an unwanted failure.

One night I stayed up until 2am praying and working through The Steps to Freedom. I flushed £150 worth of New Age medicine down the toilet; I wrote letters to those I'd hurt, asking them to forgive me; I repented of my occult past; I renounced the lies I'd been believing about myself, about God and even about Satan and his powers. I awoke the next morning completely well. In fact it wasn't until about 9am that I suddenly realised I could see clearly, I could walk unaided, my headache was gone and I actually felt "normal". Hallelujah!

Almost immediately I received a call to share the good news of what God had done in my life, and I've never looked back since. That was twelve years ago – and although I recognise that I still have a depressive tendency, especially when I'm tired, I've been equipped to recognise the enemy's strategy against my ministry and immediately take authority over my thoughts, renouncing the lies and announcing the truth.

Now, in a different area of the country, we are again applying the Freedom in Christ approach, but this time to a region! We devote much of our time to intercession and research for the Lord to show us what needs healing and setting free in the valley in which we're called to minister. We see this as a vital part of laying a good foundation for God to build His church.

In 1999 God gave me a picture of the wounded body of Christ in the area. It was an army that wanted to fight in prayer, but every time people came out of the Red Cross hut to fight, they were knocked back again by their wounds. Healing was the answer. Since then, we have used The Steps as a regular part of our one-to-one discipleship work and have also run the Freedom in Christ Discipleship Course. Through this we are seeing a growing number of individuals set free from prevailing bondages – some going back 30 years – all of whom are then being catapulted to the front line of God's army of intercessors. As the enemy's resistance grows, these troops are equipped to stand without getting knocked back. Praise God!

I can truly say that, next to finding Jesus as my Saviour, entering into the fullness of my spiritual freedom in Christ has been the most significant event of my life. I thoroughly recommend it.

Marie and Tim now have a fruitful, significant ministry applying the Freedom in Christ approach not just to individuals but on a wider level.

In my experience, God delights in taking those who are the most downtrodden and completely turning them around. It's as if He's determined to bring more good out of their lives than there has been bad. He really is the God of the turnaround – the more apparently hopeless the case, the more He loves to turn it around.

Laura's story

"My aunt fixed me with a stony disapproving stare – a look of contemptuous disapproval..."

I suppose, on the whole, my childhood was a happy one. I enjoyed school, did well there, and had lots of friends. Ours was a Christian home and I was taken to church regularly from babyhood. On the surface all seemed well-balanced and secure; however, one of my earliest memories is of a vague feeling that I was being picked on – a feeling that made me want to run away.

The truth is that there was somebody who was casting a long shadow over my otherwise sunny childhood; this was an aunt who visited us regularly, and later came to live with us. One incident that happened very early on in my life has stayed in my memory ever since. I must have been about three years old at the time, and was playing happily. Suddenly my aunt came into the room, and no sooner had she appeared than she fell over onto the floor. She might have tripped over a toy that I had left there, though I was left with a vivid memory of the particular toy she mentioned being on the sofa all the time.

Anyway, she made a huge fuss about it, saying that I had left the toy out deliberately for her to fall over, and that I was a wicked child. Her angry words burned themselves into my mind. And despite my mother's attempts to assure me that it had been an accident (which, of course, I knew already) I felt totally bewildered and terrified. I listened with horror as the adults began to discuss whether they should send for a doctor to examine my aunt...

When I was eleven years old, I went on a youth-group

weekend camp. There was something in the Bible studies that weekend that intrigued me. Someone later said she had noticed how intently I was listening as the discussion progressed. Each study lasted one hour and was on the Lord's Prayer. What impressed me most was how much could be learned from the two words "Our Father". God really spoke to me that weekend and, as a result, I committed my life to Jesus. I knew that I was now a child of God.

It was around this time, as I was beginning to grow up and go through the confusing time of young teenage years, that my aunt came to live with us. She was a difficult lady, very strong-willed and always sure she was right about everything. We did not get on at all. With the wisdom of hindsight, and from an adult perspective, I realise that she had some problems of her own. But at the tender age of thirteen I did not see it.

Although I can't recall many specific incidents, my aunt and I had several flashpoints. She openly favoured my sister, although fortunately Sally wasn't living at home much then. It seemed to me that Sally could do nothing wrong, whereas I could do nothing right. Other than that, I suspect these disagreements were probably over typically teenage matters, such as differing tastes in music, though I was never a rebel or a tearaway. One of the few incidences I can actually remember is of listening to music, and enjoying dancing to it in the family lounge. My aunt was sitting in the room – something she habitually chose to do rather than using her own sitting room. She didn't actually ask me to turn off the music, or to stop dancing; instead she fixed me with a stony, disapproving stare – a look of contemptuous disapproval.

This disapproval seemed to me to be constant. It seemed to lie behind most of our disagreements, and I could sense it as well as see it in her face. Just occasionally she said that she did love me. But her actions and body language said something different. If I was hurt or upset by an action of my aunt and let it show, she told me I was being silly or babyish. Likewise, when I watched a sad film that moved me to tears I felt disapproved of, stupid and embarrassed. I didn't feel accepted as "me" and I couldn't be myself.

As a result I became emotionally withdrawn, usually only allowing myself to cry when alone in my room. I rarely cried in front of anyone else, as I feared being ridiculed and belittled. Consequently I felt lonely and alone even though I had a good number of friends. So I buried my feelings and pretended that things didn't matter, even though deep down I was hurting desperately. I became very good at this kind of cover-up, even fooling myself into thinking I was OK when I wasn't. I discovered a "front-line" method of not expressing hurt or upset, which involved digging my nails into my hands until they hurt and left marks. That way I could concentrate on the pain in my hand and distract myself from crying.

After a few years of this, my aunt moved out and lived in nursing accommodation until she finally died. As for me, I got good qualifications, held down a responsible job and was, on the surface at least, a typical young person. But the consequences of my aunt's continued disapproval followed me into adult life. The emotional scars and the pain I had stifled continued to eat away at me inside.

Events came to a head during a very stressful and unsettling period at work and the lengthy breakdown of a friendship. I had known Debbie since our school days, and we had been good friends for many years. I could never be sure exactly what went wrong; maybe we were growing apart anyway, as does sometimes happen during one's formative years. Anyway, I felt very insecure about not having many really close friends, and another mutual friend, Jane, seemed to want Debbie's company more than she wanted mine. The result was that I felt rejected and alone and afraid that I would lose Debbie's friendship. I thought it would be entirely my fault if that happened.

In fact, there was fault on the part of all three of us, but Debbie blamed me entirely for acting out of jealousy when I pointed this out. She defended Jane, and insisted we keep asking her to join us whenever we went out – even though Jane would rarely come with us if she knew I was going to be there too. I soon began to feel very guilty and ashamed as I began to believe that it was I who was behaving unreasonably. And, in any case, Debbie kept telling me this was so. I soon felt obligated to Debbie, as she was still my friend, and I believed I had to make up for my behaviour.

I now began to read horoscopes, drawn into their lure by my desperation to make sense of what was happening. And I found myself believing what they said, as they often seemed to be very apt. However, my friendship with Debbie gradually deteriorated over the course of a year and, as I felt that she had also rejected me for being "me", I withdrew even deeper into myself.

This series of events caused the buried pain to resurface, and after a year of emotional torment I was eventually diagnosed with deep clinical depression. I was prescribed various antidepressants, which I took for many years. Around this time I left my job, as I had no self-esteem and no confidence. I would cry for hours at a time, the depth of pain becoming almost physical in its intensity. A sheer emptiness overwhelmed me. It seemed there was absolutely no hope for me. I had, in effect, stopped living.

More than once I seriously considered suicide. I remember holding a packet of tablets in my hand one night, intent on taking them all. The only thing that prevented me from doing so was the thought that they might not be enough to kill me.

Someone had earlier recommended that I go for Christian counselling, which I did for a year or so. This, coupled with the support of friends at my new church, slowly gave me a little confidence, even enabling me to go back to work in a new job. On the good days I managed fine, but on bad days I would still get very upset. Although I had progressed from being in a state of very deep depression to something approaching stability, the depression was still ongoing and was eating away at me inside.

It was during an "up" time that I met my husband and before long we decided to get married, but it seemed that almost straight away life became more difficult. This was not in any way my husband's fault. But it was as if God was saying, "You're in a safe environment now, so it's time to sort this depression out once and for all", whereupon the devil, knowing his time was short, really piled on the pressure. Things began to get worse spiritually, and I started to experience demonic visions and attacks: I was convinced that God didn't love me; I found it very hard to read my Bible or to pray; and eventually it was difficult even being in church let alone concentrating on what was being said.

With the support of friends who had sensed something was wrong months before, I went through the traditional form of deliverance ministry – the casting-out of demons. These sessions were intense and violent. I had previously thought that in such situations the person being delivered from a demon knew nothing about what was happening to them during "deliverance". I thought that they were virtually in a state of unconsciousness. This, however, was not the case. I knew exactly what was happening and felt unable to control it, so I found the sessions traumatic and terrifying.

I did talk to a couple of experienced friends in the church and also to my minister, who advised, supported and prayed with and for me, but I was still terrorised by satanic attack. I was a slave to fear and compulsions. The habit of digging my nails into my hands led to other forms of self-harm. I dug sharp objects into my arms. I tied electric cables around my neck and tightened them. I tied myself up and masturbated compulsively, believing I deserved to be beaten and raped. I felt utterly humiliated and degraded. I was convinced I was worthless, and "voices" in my head confirmed it. I hated myself and I thought I deserved everything that was happening to me. I believed absolutely that demons would destroy me.

It was at this point that I was given a leaflet about a "Living Free in Christ" conference. The speaker was a Dr Neil T. Anderson, of whom I'd never heard. And, frankly, I didn't want to hear him speak either. However, since the friend who'd given me the leaflet believed it would be helpful, and as my husband and I trusted his judgment, we both went. As an aside, just before the conference I had taken a job, feeling sure that God wanted me to be in that post. As it turned out, I hated the job, but it did mean that I was working every day of the conference, which was held in the evenings. I am convinced that this was God's way of protecting me, because it would have been quite impossible for me to be on my own at home during that time.

At the conference itself, I took in very little of what Dr Anderson said. To be honest, I didn't actually hear much of it. I was hearing those inner voices again, and they were saying, "I don't want to be here. I don't like it here..." However, I did hear just enough to know that going through The Steps to Freedom in Christ might possibly help. I contacted a local church that offered freedom appointments and set the wheels in motion for an appointment.

Those few weeks of waiting for the appointment to take place were awful. I had a vision that I was chained to the wall in a locked cell so deep inside a dungeon that I could never be found. (My husband, incidentally, had a vision that Jesus was storming through that same dungeon, flinging open the doors to reach me.) Satan turned the heat up to maximum, trying every avenue to stop me from going to the appointment. As well as self-harming, as I had before the conference, I was now convinced the freedom appointment was not going to work; that Jesus would not actually set me free, as I was too bad a person for even Jesus to want to help. That He would abandon me and that I would end up in an even worse state than before, and would then belong to Satan for ever. But I did go to the appointment. God had provided His loving protection and support to get me that far in the form of my long-suffering husband and a couple of faithful friends.

I shall never ever forget the appointment. The two ladies who were helping me through the Steps to Freedom (one leading the appointment, the other there to pray for me) reassured me that all I said would be in strict confidence. There was no need to feel ashamed or embarrassed about anything at all. God showed me those areas in my life that I needed to deal with, the sins I needed to confess and renounce, and the people I needed to forgive, then it was up to me to pray through everything God had shown me. I had to choose to follow His ways and to believe His word and not to rely on how I felt. The forgiveness prayer was probably the longest, especially as I had to allow suppressed pain to surface, and to allow myself to feel it as I forgave. I sobbed my way through some of this prayer. But I also saw Jesus sitting with me, encouraging me and urging me on. Now, when I think of how I saw Jesus at that point, I am still overwhelmed all over again at the thought of God's kindness and love.

Finally, I was able to forgive my aunt for all the damage she had caused in me – even for the accusation that I was a "wicked child". I was encouraged to choose truth, and helped to see where I believed a lie. For example, if I was believing that God could not love me – he loved everyone else but me! – one of my helpers would say: "Is that true? Or is it one of

Satan's lies? God says you are honoured and precious in His sight, and He loves you" (Isaiah 43:4).

The whole process was very, very gentle and very effective. Jesus led me out of that cell I'd seen in the vision, and He set me free from depression and from the problems that had caused it. I can read my Bible and pray easily now, free from voices in my head. I no longer harm myself, though I had to be very alert to the danger times, especially in the early weeks following the appointment. And I had to stop myself from following the habit of harming myself and instead ask God to help me cope. Sometimes I have failed, but I know now that it is just a setback, that I am not condemned for it but simply need to pray through it and move on.

I would emphasise that this is no miracle fix-everything cure. It had been, and still is, ongoing discipleship. I still need to take my responsibility and continue walking in the freedom gained for me by Jesus' victory over Satan at Calvary. It is up to me to choose the truth of God's word daily, as it can be all too easy to start thinking along the same lines that I did before my appointment. I need to be especially alert to my own particular areas of vulnerability and "catch" thoughts as they occur, to ensure I do not believe something that is untrue. Of course I still have my "off" days, as everyone does. But I now know how to deal with them, and they are nothing like as bad as they once were.

Depression doesn't control me any more. Finding my freedom in Christ has changed my life.

In this chapter we've seen how two Christians escaped from depression by closing the doors in their lives that were open to the enemy (repentance) and choosing to believe the truth (faith). There is nothing new in this approach – repentance and faith in Christ have always been the answer and always will be.

Can all depression be cured this way? Depression can have a

number of causes. Most agree that the roots of bipolar (manic) depression, for example, are primarily physical. Appropriate drugs are likely to be effective here. However, most of the depression in our society is what medical professionals call "unipolar" and is caused either by a sense of loss (real or perceived) or by a learned sense of helplessness and hopelessness, often compounded by the enemy's lies. In these cases, when sufferers connect with the truth that they have everything they need in Christ and that in Christ they are absolutely not helpless or hopeless, then things start to change.

Counselling

Laura's story, in particular, raises important questions regarding how we help those who are struggling.

Why did Laura not find her freedom through counselling? Counselling can be valuable, but if the counsellor ignores the reality of the spiritual world or simply does not believe that problems such as Laura's can be completely resolved, then they will merely settle for giving her strategies for coping with their negative effects, rather than seeing them dealt with once and for all. Through the Steps to Freedom process, Laura was able to bring her troubles directly to Jesus Christ, who is the Wonderful Counsellor, and see Him resolve them.

Increasingly, I am coming across Christian counsellors who use The Steps to Freedom when they are counselling Christians. One told me that it has completely revolutionised her approach because, rather than having people come back week after week, she is finding that after a relatively short time they are saying that they don't need to keep coming back because their issues are resolved. This could, of course, have a negative effect on her business! However, she has found that precisely the opposite is true, because word soon gets round and more clients than she can cope with ask to see her.

Deliverance ministry

Why did Laura not find her freedom through the casting-out of demons in a power encounter? I would never denigrate an approach to ministry used by others, especially if it is bearing fruit. I would say, however, that I have never found it necessary to resort to "casting out" a demon in the sense that I (the deliverer) deal directly with the demon. That is not to say that Christians do not need delivering from problems in which a demon is involved. However, the issue is not power but truth. In a "truth encounter" such as The Steps to Freedom in Christ, all you have to do is work with the person themselves and encourage them to choose to believe and act on the truth. The power of Satan is in the lie and exposing the lie to the truth is what brings freedom.

I know that Jesus and Paul both practised the power-encounter form of deliverance where they addressed the demon directly, but only with people who were not Christians. Those who practise this approach today sometimes wonder why there are no instructions in the New Testament for how to go about delivering a Christian from demonic influence. I would argue that there are:

> **Submit yourselves, then, to God. Resist the devil, and he will flee from you. (James 4:7)**

However, it's the person with the problem who has to do the submitting and resisting. Although I can support and encourage them, I can't do it for them. However, if they submit themselves to God by repenting, when they resist the devil he has no option but to go quietly because the grounds he had for influencing the person have been taken away. That is why The Steps to Freedom is a calm, gentle process.

There is no need to get into a dogfight with the enemy in which the demon and the deliverer battle it out, leaving the poor affected person like a pawn in our game. I love Neil Anderson's illustration of this – if you have a problem with flies in your kitchen, you could study them carefully, work out where they were coming from and pick them off one by one. What would happen? More would come! Why? Because there's a big, rotten, stinking pile of rubbish attracting them. So what's the best way to sort out the problem? Get rid of the rubbish! In other words, deal with the sin that is the root cause rather than with the demonic influence, which is simply a consequence of a lack of repentance.

Suggestions for further reading

- *Finding Hope Again* (Anderson & Baumchen, Regal, 1999)
- *Overcoming Depression* (N. & J. Anderson, Regal, 2004).

Available from your local Christian bookshop or directly from Freedom in Christ Ministries.

Chapter 7

Freedom from deeper problems

We've already heard from many who have found freedom from serious problems in their lives. In this chapter we'll hear from Jennifer, who suffered from a condition that used to be called "multiple personality disorder" and nowadays tends to be called "Dissociative Identity Disorder", or DID for short.

DID is a God-given defence mechanism that enables people who suffer traumatic abuse to cope and even live a somewhat normal life, at least on the outside.

Here is Jennifer's explanation of the condition:

It is difficult for most people to understand, although to some extent we all dissociate at times – such as when we switch off from what is going on around us to focus on a TV programme or phone call.

Dissociative Identity Disorder begins in early childhood as a response to trauma, and is a coping mechanism that helps some children to survive what would otherwise be too much to bear. The child learns to dissociate from the situation that is causing pain and creates a separate identity or "alter" (which means "other"), who comes to the surface while the painful situation is occurring and then goes away again. The child can then continue as though the trauma had not taken place. As the child grows, he or she will often learn to use this means of escape in any difficult situation. Many "alters" can be created, but the child remains totally unaware of their existence. There are varying degrees of severity and complexity, and each person is different, partly depending on the kind of abuse or trauma he or she has survived. It is usually in adulthood that the walls of amnesia begin to crumble and the separate parts can no longer hide from the main person. It's a bit like a Russian doll. Sometimes the outer doll will step back and one of the little ones from inside will step forward and take over for a while.

When I first came across DID, I saw a mature woman switch before my eyes into a four-year-old girl, as if someone had simply changed the software in a computer. It was an unnerving experience. I suddenly found myself talking to a child in the body of the previously completely normal woman. Yet the voice, the language, the body language and the emotions were all those of a four-year-old. (You can read that story in *Am I a Good Girl Yet?* by Carolyn Bramhall, Monarch, 2005.)

Let's read Jennifer's story and then look a little more at this subject.

Jennifer's story

"It was as if a child within was speaking in my place, expressing buried pain, fear or anger..."

A little girl is sitting at the top of the stairs in the dark. She is holding a pink rabbit tightly in her arms, and rocking her body backwards and forwards. Downstairs, she can hear her parents arguing. There is shouting and screaming, and sometimes the sound of breaking crockery – plates and cups being smashed against a wall. She clutches her rabbit even more tightly, and squeezes her eyes shut. As she gets older, she forms the habit of staying up late to watch horror films so that she can be the last one to climb the stairs...

Many years later, she is in bed waiting for her husband to come up; she can hear him below in a heated argument with a colleague. She starts to pray as fear begins to clutch at her. Suddenly she sits up in bed and cries out in the voice of a child:

"Please stop it! Mummy and Daddy – please stop it!"

All of us are on a journey, and on the way it is good when other Christians come alongside to help us take the next step forward. There have been many who have helped me along my journey and some of those have been members of Freedom in Christ Ministries. To all these folk I am truly grateful.

I had become familiar with some of Neil Anderson's books, having read *Victory over the Darkness* and *The Bondage Breaker*. We had also worked through other books in our mid-week study group. I had dealt with many concerns in my life, and my husband and I were both in leadership in our fellowship. Outwardly, there did not seem to be any problems. But during a special "Setting Your Church Free" weekend for elders and their wives, God began to speak to me in a special way. Steve Goss from Freedom in Christ led the weekend and as he spoke it was as if God started to unlock some things that had been hidden inside for a long time.

Steve was careful to make sure everyone had opportunities to speak, and this was very important. During one of the sessions, he invited us to share something that had hurt us in our fellowship. As I began to speak about something I had already worked through, I was surprised by the intensity of the pain that suddenly came to the surface and I could not continue. I felt like a helpless little child, trying to understand what had happened. Some others in the group suggested that I had not forgiven the people concerned, but I knew this was not the case.

During the year that followed, similar situations arose with increasing regularity. I would be fine one moment, but then find I could not suppress some very strong feelings that would take me by surprise. It was as if a child within was speaking in my place, expressing buried pain, fear or anger. I had experienced similar emotions rising to the surface before, but this time someone had taken the lid off and I couldn't get it back on again.

As a child, I was very timid, shy and fearful. Both my parents were deeply rejected people and so they found it very difficult to express love and affection for their own children. They married because they "had to" and they did not really want a family. Each child brought more stress, pain and financial worry rather than joy. My mother was also mentally ill and so was emotionally very unstable. The medication that she was taking meant that she would have dramatic mood swings, and often she would spend days in bed in the dark, very depressed and unwilling to communicate with anyone. We learned to avoid upsetting her because my father would become very angry and blame us whenever she was depressed, as he did not know how else to cope. She would then be bitterly angry with him. They did their best to provide for us, but their own emotional tanks were empty.

Children learn to adapt to difficult situations and to cope somehow, but all the while they are forming a belief system about themselves and the world, based on their experiences rather than on objective truth. I didn't know my mother was ill when I was small, and I had no concept of what mothers and fathers are supposed to be like. But we all have an inbuilt need for affection and warmth and emotional nurture. I don't remember ever being read a story, being hugged or being told I was special. Most of the words I heard were negative. I don't have major traumatic memories, but there were several incidents where I was afraid and there was no one there to protect or comfort me. Eye contact is very important and children get their sense of identity from how others see them: but eye contact is difficult for someone who is depressed. I grew up thinking I was a nuisance, stupid, not worthy of love – and ugly. I should have been a boy. Everything was somehow my fault.

When I was about four, we were playing in the park. (We were often sent out to play, which was healthy of course. But we had no choice, and it added to the feeling that we didn't belong.) My oldest sister saw some boys from school and said they were bullies, and that we had to climb over the gate to get away. We panicked, and left our toys on the grass. The boys came over and threw the toys into the trees, and then their father came and called them away. When they had gone, and we ventured back over the gate, I discovered that my favourite toy – my panda – was missing. I was very upset, and tried to persuade my sisters to go and get help from the boys' father. When they refused, I went by myself. As I ran I called out, "They lost my panda!" but the father shrugged and walked away.

At home, my mother promised to buy a new panda, but she never did. I didn't want a new one. It upset me to think of my poor panda, cold and lonely in the tree. My parents had no time or energy to go and look for the toy. Their patience never lasted long, and they would become angry if we were upset. They didn't know how to cope with their own pain, let alone ours. I learned several things through that incident: boys are bullies; there is no point in asking grown-ups to help; parents make promises they don't keep; and if you get upset, Mum and Dad will get angry, so it's best to keep it to yourself.

Years later, I read a story to my children about a boy who had lost his favourite toy. Every time I read it I would feel this tremendous pain from inside, and I had to hide the fact that I had tears streaming down my face. The little girl inside of me was still hurting because that wound had never been healed – just buried.

When I became aware of my mother's illness, I felt I had to hide it because I was ashamed. My friends called the local mental hospital "the loony bin" and our school choir would sometimes go there to sing to the patients. I was alarmed by some of the behaviour we witnessed and I was afraid that I was somehow linked to these people through my mother. As a student I used to say "I think I'm going mad" several times a day, until I realised, and trained myself to stop. But there was always an underlying fear that I would do so.

I had no one to talk to about the things that worried or upset me, and so I kept everything locked up inside. I remember, when I was six, having to stay with strangers while my parents went to look at houses. We had no relatives or friends who could look after us. My younger sister was screaming and having tantrums, and I stood watching other children playing outside through the windows. The people were kind, and tried to persuade me to go out, but I was too afraid. More and more I withdrew into my own world for safety. I loved to read and make up stories, and my dream world became my place of refuge. I remember sometimes, when I was very afraid, watching myself from a safe distance as if I was no longer in my own body, but somehow detached from it, hovering nearby. I began to live my life as though watching through an imaginary window, always carefully weighing up what to say and do, according to how afraid I would be.

We moved, and I went to a new school. Although it was good in many ways, I felt like an outsider. We were poorer than most families, and I hated the days when we could wear our own clothes instead of uniform. At my next school, like most teenagers I became very self-conscious, and there were many things I hated about myself. I often just wished I could disappear.

When I was 16 my mother had another breakdown, and I sat on the bed for hours, rocking backwards and forwards, when I was supposed to be revising for exams. I was quite clever, though, and managed to do well. Work became my way of achieving some sense of purpose, and I became a perfectionist, always striving to do better and never satisfied with my own efforts. I never thought I had done enough to feel good about myself.

Decisions were always very difficult to make. I had grown up in an atmosphere in which emotional manipulation was normal, so I would try to work out what other people wanted me to do. I would have internal arguments over whether it was safe to agree to something as simple as playing a game of Scrabble, and often I would just say "no" as it was easier, and then think about it afterwards.

I actually changed my degree course to take a subject I was not so good at because the professor had tried to be nice to me. She told me my headmistress had told her about my mother, and then she put her arm around me and assured me that they would look after me. I could not cope with physical contact and, although I smiled, inside I wanted to run a mile. I later thought of all sorts of good reasons why I should do a different course, and even stood up to my teachers when they tried to dissuade me. It was only years later that I realised why I did that.

At 18 I became a Christian, and for the first time in my life I knew somebody loved me, and that I belonged. I took a year out before going to university to work with children, and during that year I had the wonderful experience of being filled with the Holy Spirit. I went to a really good church, where I had some very good teaching. I saw God answer prayer in amazing ways, and my faith grew and grew as I learned to depend on Him for everything. It really was like walking out of a dark place into the light.

As a student I was still on fire, and did some training with an evangelistic organisation. Gradually the love of Jesus replaced the lies I had come to believe, and gave me hope for the future, and the ability to love others. After university I knew I wanted to serve God full-time, although I was still struggling with fear and low self-esteem. I was also hiding an eating disorder, and my family were all going through crises. I was advised to get involved in a local church and start from there, so I went home. One of my sisters had tried to take her own life and things were very difficult at home, but I felt I should be there to try and bring the love of Jesus into the situation. I wanted to be part of the solution, not part of the problem.

However, I was very immature emotionally, and still related to adults in the mode of a child. It was not until some years later, after the birth of two children, that I first felt like an adult myself. I was at a Bible week and someone who was praying for me suddenly said: "God has shown me that you are like a twelve-year-old girl, and He is going to 'grow you up' emotionally."

I was a bit stunned, but ten minutes later I wanted to shout it aloud: "I'm grown up!" Because, for the first time in my life, I knew what it was to feel like an adult, although it didn't work in all situations...

To return to my story, I got a job and became very involved in my local church. Jack, the pastor, was like a father to me. He was highly respected, and many people besides me benefited from his ministry. I knew that God was my Father, and I didn't feel the need of any other father figure; but at the time some people were teaching that rejected people needed to be part of an extended family. Jack encouraged me to open up to him and gradually I began to trust him enough to share some of my darkest fears and pain.

After some time, however, this man began to abuse me. I was shocked and frightened, and I froze. We are told that our instinct in times of danger is "fight or flight". My way of running was to act as if nothing was happening. I would disconnect from the situation until it was over. As if it was happening to someone else... At first he apologised, and promised never to do it again. And I believed him. Soon, however, I realised he was not going to stop, and my heart sank in dismay. He always asked God to forgive him afterwards; and then he began to pray: "Forgive us..." This really confused me, and I began to believe I was also guilty.

I suppose I had become too dependent on his fatherly affection, and it was hard for me to live in denial of pain, hiding secrets: but I hated what he was doing. I also knew that to tell anyone would mean he would lose his position, and I was used to feeling responsible for the well-being of the adults in my life. Besides, I had promised not to tell. I knew what he was doing was wrong, but I had been taught that all sin is the same in God's eyes. I did not realise that there are always consequences and that if we sow bad seed there will always be a bitter harvest – either in our own lives or in the lives of those we sin against.

I did try to get advice, but none of it was helpful. On one occasion I was in a car with a trusted friend of Jack's, trying to pluck up courage to tell him. For about an hour he talked, while I had a fierce internal argument going on inside my head. I was just about to say "Can I ask you something?" when he said, "Well, I'd better go now." I felt as if I had struggled up the side of a steep well, only to slip back down again. I didn't try to share it again. My only hope was that God would rescue me, and I prayed fervently that He would do so. But it seemed to me as if He had abandoned me.

It was easy for my old belief system to replace what I had come to believe as a Christian. I was a failure; I had let God down, so I was now worthless to Him. I had missed His purpose for my life and it was all my fault. I believed the Bible, and I didn't doubt His faithfulness and love – I simply adjusted my interpretation of what those words meant. His love now seemed distant and impersonal, and closeness was for special people, not for failures like me. I continued to serve in the church, and live in denial of what was happening. Somehow God still seemed to use me in ministry, but inside my heart was broken.

Later, I married and had a family. Things were difficult for us, but we were both determined to work through things God's way. At a weekend for married couples I finally opened up about what had happened with Jack. It was helpful because it explained some of our problems. But the counsellors, and some others I shared with later, assumed I had been a willing participant, and this added to my feelings of guilt rather than dealing with them.

A few years later I had some very significant ministry at a healing centre. It was there that I began to understand why I had reacted as I did, and that I was able to forgive myself and receive God's forgiveness and healing. I understood that as a child I had learned to bury my pain, and to separate off memories and even parts of my personality as a way of coping with traumatic events. This is sometimes called Dissociative Identity Disorder, or DID. I began to believe that God had not rejected me after all, and that He still had a purpose for my life. I still wanted to serve Him full-time and was very excited when He called me to leave work and step out in faith in a new venture.

Someone said that most of us are like onions. God will peel off a layer and we think we are OK. But then later on He will go a bit deeper and do some more work in our hearts. After I had been to the Freedom in Christ conference things began to fall apart. On the one hand, God was leading me into new areas of ministry; but on the other I was having real problems physically and emotionally and I began to doubt whether I had heard Him correctly. In the weeks and months that followed, I found that there was a group of people with whom I would suddenly feel like a child, and very powerful emotions – usually fear – would surface at illogical moments. I would get upset over silly things, and no amount of forgiving, repenting and other tested methods of release were any help. On one occasion, I cried for three hours because someone was annoyed with me. I knew it was a huge overreaction, but I could not control the fear. It came from the little girl who was terrified of making her parents angry. Some parts of me still had not grown up.

The physical problems I was having became a real hindrance to my work, but pointed to underlying problems which really needed to be seen and treated in order that I would not have more difficulties in that area later. This really was like a picture of what God had been doing in my heart. For two years I had struggled and coped with brokenness inside. But now God was allowing it to surface so that He could bring me to a place of greater healing and wholeness. The only way to do this was to take away some of my defences. I thought at the time that it was a disaster, but the consequence has been to encourage me to seek and find more truth and freedom.

The year after the conference I was planning to join a team of people who could take others through The Steps to Freedom. But to do this I would first need to go through The Steps myself. I was watching a training video and heard Neil Anderson mention DID, so I knew it was something that Freedom in Christ people were aware of. Our pastor also mentioned hearing a story of someone who had suffered from the same thing and had been helped by the Freedom in Christ approach. Not only had she been helped, but she was now working for Freedom in Christ, advising church leaders. After a very difficult leaders' meeting, during which I had become very upset and uncommunicative, I recognised that this was indeed the problem, and decided I needed some help.

This time, instead of going away to a healing centre where

I could be anonymous, it seemed right to share what was happening with my pastor, Stuart, and try to explain it to some of the people in our fellowship.

Stuart contacted the Freedom in Christ office, who suggested we meet with Carolyn. We went with two friends, Jane and Sarah. This was a very helpful meeting and gave us all an understanding of what was happening, and how we could begin to work through it. I felt very safe with Carolyn because she understood how I was feeling and gave me hope that there was a way through. She recognised that the "alter" needed to feel safe enough to surface, and share things she had been keeping hidden for so long, and her gentle encouragement and patience allowed this to happen during the meeting. I then began to meet regularly with Jane, and we kept in touch with Carolyn for ongoing support when we needed it. I also continued to meet with Sarah to pray. It was important for some people in my own fellowship to know what was happening this time, so that I would have ongoing support.

First of all I went through The Steps to Freedom with Stuart and Jane from my church. It gave me confidence to know that they understood dissociation, as I knew that "alters" often surface in stressful situations, and The Steps can be stressful! People with "alters" have already spent a long time trying to repent of and renounce the negative feelings that surface, and others may have tried to deliver them from spirits of fear, etc. An "alter" cannot be cast out or repented of because she is not a demon, she is part of the whole person. She needs to be accepted and welcomed and listened to so that she can share the burden she has been carrying, and find people. There may be a need for repentance and deliverance, but first must come understanding and acceptance.

"Alters" often have different names, and I will call this one Jenny. Each time we met, we would ask Jesus to bring Jenny to the surface, so she could share something that had upset her, or made her afraid. Like the Russian doll, I would consciously allow Jenny to surface. She was very shy and would not let Jane get too close. As the child part begins to feel safe, she will say things the adult has no recollection of. We also became aware that, although I am an adult, Jenny saw and experienced things as a child, and Jane had to relate to her as she would to a child, or she could not understand or receive what she was saying. She introduced Jenny to Jesus, so that she could tell Him all the things she needed to say, and we were often amazed at the way He would gently respond with pictures and words that brought her comfort and healing, and even laughter.

Jenny told us about how sad and lonely she was when she and the other children were sent away on holiday, to give her parents a break. She became very withdrawn, and didn't want to join in any of the games. Jane was telling her what a good friend Jesus is, and that He would be with her all the time. Jenny thought that was quite a funny idea but she wasn't that interested. Suddenly she said, "I want Him to make my mummy better!" I hadn't realised that this was what she had been so worried about. Jesus assured her He would look after her mother, and that she could go and play. She was then able to let go of the burden she had been carrying.

There were problems with friends at school – things that are important to children, but which adults often dismiss as insignificant. However, if the pain and fear remain buried, they will come out and affect us in some way. Jesus showed me a picture of Jenny on His lap, and He told her she was special, "a princess".

We also decided to go over some of the Steps with Jenny, including an extra sheet on freemasonry. The first time through there was no reaction, as I had already had ministry in this area, but there was a definite release when we went though it again with Jenny. It was very interesting, because, at the time, I was having therapy for my voice, and the therapist commented that it was as if my throat had been held in a vice for many years – which seemed to point to the rope freemasons use in their ceremonies. I am a worship leader and singing was something that was very important to Jenny. She recalled my first solo in public, when no one was there to encourage and affirm me. I also felt a sense of guilt and rejection at the time, because I was standing in for a friend who was ill, so I believed the teachers didn't really want me to sing. As an adult my motivation for singing is to serve the Lord and His people, but as Jenny began to surface it would be as if the solo had been a very recent event. It hadn't been a problem before, but after the first conference I began to find that if I sang something new I would be desperate for affirmation afterwards. Struggling with negative thoughts such as "No one really wants me to be singing, and they all wish I would be quiet!" I could not dispel these thoughts with reason. There were also some people whom I had forgiven, but whom Jenny also had to forgive specifically.

After several months, Jenny was ready to become part of the whole person, and no longer separate. At first I noticed a real improvement. I found I could be in situations where before I would have expected to feel a sense of fear or panic rising up inside me – but this did not happen. If you had asked me before whether I heard voices in my head I would have said no – because all the voices were mine. But as each "alter" that had been identified was also integrated, the intense internal arguing that I used to experience diminished. Jenny had not disappeared – she had added her personality to the whole person.

A bit later, however, I became very depressed, and this lasted for several months. I tried to work out why and put it down to all sorts of things. It was as if a gulf had opened up between me and my Father in heaven, and I was very afraid of

His anger. After a while I realised that anything Jenny had been protecting me from was no longer hidden from me, and that she had witnessed what had happened with the first pastor, Jack. Although we had made sure she had forgiven him she was still carrying fear and guilt from the way this situation had affected my relationship with God. It was time to face the pain and work through it.

Soon after the first conference, God had brought someone else into my life to bring me hope when everything seemed to be going wrong. I thought no one would trust me again because I felt as if I were falling to pieces, but a pastor called Mark, who has experience of helping people with DID, came to preach at our church. The first time he brought encouragement, and the child within knew he was bringing God's love, and began to hunger for more. In fact I cried when he left, without understanding why I was so upset. The second time he brought a word of prophecy and I had real hope that God was going to lead me through. The third time, when I was depressed, he prayed with me and helped me to see that I needed to trust God's timing rather than try to rush things. I thought I should be OK by now, but God had more to do.

I began to look at "hope" in the Bible and got as far as Job. I realised then that I needed to know what *God* thought about what had happened. I needed to know if He was angry with me. I needed to know why He had not rescued me, and whether I could trust Him to "never leave me or forsake me" as He promised. I knew there was a risk in telling others about it. People tend to look at things through their own experiences and make judgments, as Job's friends did. I was willing to confess anything in order to renew my closeness to God, but it is useless to confess something that you are not guilty of. I realised I needed to know what a father would say in that situation. Most of the counselling I had had before had been with women, and, while I do not doubt their integrity, the child in me had come to believe that women say what they think you want to hear or what will keep you quiet. Jenny wanted to hear what a father would say, however difficult it might be for her.

Mark helped me to see that I needed to explore some of the negative emotions that were surfacing, rather than just push them away. I needed to embrace the truth of God's word with my mind and spirit, but at the same time to accept these reactions and look at where they were coming from. I had been seeing responses such as fear and anger as entities that were separate from me, and renouncing them as sin, rather than seeing that they were coming from a part of me that needed healing. It was a form of self-rejection.

On one occasion I decided to explore why I had become so afraid of phoning my pastor, Stuart. I had tried renouncing the fear but that had not worked. The Holy Spirit reminded me at once of an occasion when I was about seven, in a school assembly. I watched some boys do something silly and I copied them because I wanted to be accepted by the other children. Unfortunately the headmaster saw me, and was very angry. He shouted at me, and I had to say my name twice. Then, in the classroom, the teacher told me what a disappointment I was, and that I had let down the whole class. At the time I took on board the words, but I blanked out the fear and shame. I knew they were still locked up inside and God was just allowing them to surface so that He could bring healing. I went through the usual prayers of forgiveness and asked Jesus to come into the situation. He told me I had to speak to the child part myself. This was strange, but as a parent I knew what to say. Yes, it was silly, but Jesus still loved her, and I did too. Then a child's voice responded and let out all the pain and fear she had held on to for so long. I realised this was another child part and there was more work to do. I also think this healing opened the way for me to feel safer about sharing other things that had been buried.

Soon after this, our church hosted a Freedom in Christ Ministries course, "Helping Others Find Freedom in Christ", and we went through The Steps again. Although I have always endeavoured to keep short accounts and make sure I have forgiven everyone I can think of, I was very surprised at my reaction to Step Three, the one that covers forgiveness. This time God reminded me of several things that had happened for which I had forgiven people, but now He was focusing my attention on how I had felt at the time. I had learned to bury my emotions and not allow myself to feel, but as He brought each scene to mind I began to release deep inner pain I did not know was there. Much of the pain was not over what had taken place, but rather over the love and nurture that had been missing, which had left a wound in my heart. He also showed me what I had believed about myself in those situations, and replaced the lies with the truth of how He sees me in His love for me.

For example, I remembered a time when I was about four and I got lost at the station. When my father found me I was just relieved he did not shout at me. It didn't occur to me that he could have comforted me and made me feel safe, until God showed me that I was feeling very frightened and vulnerable. There were many times when my mother had not been there for me emotionally at important times as I was growing up. I spent several hours weeping as I released that pain to Him, and He brought healing and comfort to those wounds, because He is the perfect Father.

Then I tried to pray about Jack, and I found I couldn't – because each time I tried I would suddenly become terrified of God's anger. I realised there was a deep insecurity because I had believed He had abandoned me. After several days of crying out to Him, I wrote to Mark. I had been afraid he would reject me, but now I knew I had to have an answer. So I told him my story and, as soon as I had sent it to him, I felt God's presence in a way I had not for a long time. Mark replied, assuring me that God was not angry with me, and that he did not reject me either. It is only since that time that I have realised what a deep wound it had caused and how much it had affected my relationship with the Father. The enemy had kept me bound for years by his lies about God's love, but it is *knowing* the truth that sets us free!

God has given me a special verse and I believe that I will come to a place where the Russian doll is no longer in pieces. Jeremiah 32:39 says this: "I will give them singleness of heart and action, so that they will always fear me for their own good and the good of their children after them."

One of the things that has kept me going on my journey towards wholeness is knowing that it will benefit my children. I have learned a great deal in God's family about how to love them and they have taught me so much themselves. And every time Jesus heals an old wound we are taking back ground from the enemy – ground that belongs to us.

I am still on my journey, as we all are. As a child I used to draw rivers as straight lines, but I have discovered that rivers cannot be controlled in the way that canals can. Rivers often twist and turn, and sometimes appear to be going the wrong way altogether. There are exciting places where they rush and splash and swirl over rocks and tree roots. And there are quiet, calm places where the water runs deep and still. But all the time it is moving forward, bringing life. Looking back, I can see that, even when I thought I had lost my way, and that I had been abandoned, my Father had not let go of me but was gently leading me through.

I am so grateful to everybody at Freedom in Christ Ministries who have helped me on my journey by equipping people in my church to lead me through the process. But most of all I would like to thank the Lord Jesus, who died to set me free, and my Father in heaven, who never let me go.

DID

Jennifer was struggling with some traumatic experiences from childhood. These are at the root of many people's struggles. It's important to understand, however, that people are not in bondage to the traumatic event itself but to the lies they have come to believe as a result of that event. For example, those who have been sexually abused often come to believe as a result of their experiences that they are dirty. It's that feeling of dirtiness rather than the event itself that becomes the main problem. The truth is that no child of God is dirty any more – we have been washed completely clean by the blood of Jesus. Their healing comes when they are able to recognise the lie and start to believe the truth.

Jennifer's dissociation was designed to protect her from looking at the truth of what actually happened because it was too painful for her to face. However, when you know who you are in Christ, that you are loved and accepted unconditionally, that you are completely safe in God's hands, then all that can change. At that point, it's possible to look at what happened from the position of who you are now rather than who you were then. No matter what happened, or how awful the trauma or the shame, the truth that you are now a child of God, who can come boldly into His presence at any time, perfectly clean, loved and accepted, makes all the difference. You are not a product of your past experiences. You are a product of what Christ accomplished on the cross. Satan does not own you any more and he cannot have you back.

I have had the privilege of seeing many deeply wounded Christians change as they come to understand just who they are in Christ. It's a delight to see them come to the fantastic realisation that they don't any longer have to drag their past around with them like a ball and chain.

As was the case with Jennifer, it takes some time for them to work through the issues and learn to renew their minds – usually a matter of several months – and they benefit hugely from being in a church that supports them as they do this.

More Christians live with DID than you might realise. It's a God-given mechanism to protect us during severe trauma as children. However, it begins to break down during adulthood and can cause problems. The truth is that an adult Christian with DID doesn't need this defence mechanism any more. Christ is their defence. In Christ the barriers that have been built in the mind can come down and the person can become whole. The answer is the same – repentance and faith – but it can take longer for a person with these deeper problems.

Jennifer found her freedom in the context of her own church, even though those helping her had no experience of DID. Their confidence that Jennifer could expect to resolve all her problems in Christ was helped by the contact they had with Carolyn from Freedom in Christ Ministries. Carolyn leads a team called "Walking with the Wounded", whose purpose is quite simply to walk alongside church leaders as they go through the process of leading a hurting person into complete freedom in their church. That, after all, is the very best place a hurting person could be as they wrestle with deep issues.

I know from personal experience what it is like to be faced with trying to help a hurting person when you have no previous experience of the matters at hand and no particular expertise. It can be an uncomfortable place to be. I've every admiration for leaders like Stuart who choose not to simply avoid the hurting person but to take a step of faith and instead choose to help.

If you are a leader faced with helping someone with more deeply rooted problems, the main thing you need is faith that the Gospel really works, a real compassion for the hurting person and some basic biblical principles. For example, it's important to understand that you can't "fix" anyone. All you can do is encourage them to come to Jesus who is the Wonderful Counsellor and act on everything He has given them. You can't forgive for them, repent for them or have faith for them. All you can do is be there for them and keep pointing them to Jesus.

The first time I helped someone in my own church with these kinds of troubles I e-mailed colleagues in the States and asked for advice. I think the best advice I got was simply this: "Don't worry; Jesus always turns up." Indeed He did. It was a great relief to me when I understood that my role is simply to connect the hurting person to Jesus.

I have now seen many apparently "hopeless cases" walk to freedom with the loving help and support of their church, who in turn are supported by a member of Freedom in Christ's Walking with the Wounded team.

Sexual matters

In common with many, Jennifer was sexually abused. Satan seems to take advantage of sexual sin more than any other. The stronghold is greater if the abuser is an authority figure, such as a church leader as in Jennifer's case, but especially if the abuser is a parent.

We have found it necessary for all sexual sins to be renounced. During Step 6, people ask the Lord to show them all their past sexual sins and partners, whether they were a willing participant or not. Of course, He shows them. When they renounce those experiences, they break the wrong bonds that were formed. The power of Satan and sin has been broken and now they need simply to renew their minds and realise, as mentioned above, that they are not products of their past experiences but of what Jesus did for them on the cross. They are as clean and pure as if those bad experiences had never taken place.

Yet again, we see Jesus come and completely resolve these problems!

Suggestions for further reading

- *Set Free* (Anderson, Monarch, 2003)
- *Finding Freedom in a Sex-Obsessed World* (Anderson, Harvest House, 2004)

- *Am I a Good Girl Yet?* (Bramhall, Monarch, 2005).

Available from your local Christian bookshop or directly from Freedom in Christ Ministries.

Chapter 8

Freedom from addiction

Addiction issues have featured in a number of the stories we've heard so far. Richie and Susie illustrate how even the most apparently hopeless cases can resolve their problems and find their freedom in Christ.

Richie and Susie's story

"When Richie was not in prison, we lived in the same house, but were never actually together. Richie would be upstairs having his buzz on heroin, while Susie would be downstairs having her buzz on cannabis…"

Richie begins the story:

I was born in Glasgow in 1952. Before I was born my father was a foundry labourer but he did not work after my birth for 20 years! I was the fifth of eight children, living in a four-bed-roomed house, dependent on Social Security. My father was an alcoholic but he lived in denial. He was a Jekyll-and-Hyde character. When sober, he was a quiet gentleman who did little to help the household and was usually riddled with guilt for what he had done after the last bout of drinking. My mother was everything a mother should be – always protective of the children, coping as best she could.

We children all lived in fear of our father. I became a thief, and if he found out what I had been stealing he would wait until the next dole money came through, get drunk, and then come home at two in the morning. I would wake, fighting for breath and find that he had his hands round my throat. Once when I was caught stealing, he dragged me across the room, threatening to put my hand in the electric light socket. He then took a knife and threatened to cut my hands off. One of his favourite sports was to start a boxing match with us boys so that we ended up punching each other, and punching him. Once, when I was about eleven, he punched me back so hard I was knocked to the ground.

The violence seemed to start when the normal course of discipline failed. There was always a high level of verbal aggression and looking back I can sense his frustration as he tried to control his large and unruly family. Although he never went to church himself, he would insist on my mother and all the children going every Sunday.

One particularly unpleasant memory is being asked at the age of six to show a friend of my father's to the toilet. He made me hold him while he urinated. My father could see there was something wrong with me when we came back and asked me what had happened. After I went to bed, I heard a huge row going on, and I remember feeling vindicated. In that way my father always stood up for his family, but it was the way he dealt with us that left scars. At the age of twelve I had long hair over my eyes and he told me to comb it back. When I went outside I pulled it down again and he noticed it. That night he hacked it off using a knife as well as scissors, leaving ugly bald patches at the front of my head. I felt utterly humiliated.

I was fourteen when I took my first drink: a friend and I stole a flagon of cider! I remember clearly the feeling of confidence that swept through me after that drink. The lights in the shops suddenly seemed brighter and the whole world became an attractive place to me. I never seemed to stop drinking after that. Sometimes I bought it; sometimes I broke into pubs and stole it. But from then on never a week went by without a drink.

At fifteen I was sent to an approved school for 16 months, and during that time I drank openly and excessively. By the age of 17 I was drinking with alcoholics in the toilets of Glasgow when I should have been at work. Approved school had at least got me out of the house and made me feel tough. But the next stop was borstal. I had assaulted four or five police officers and this was their response when they had overpowered me, so to theft and alcohol I now added violence. When I came out of borstal I went to work in hotels in Scotland, but my drinking became worse. While working on the Isle of Man I met a girl called Catherine and we got into a relationship, which ended in her becoming pregnant. I took her back to Scotland, where we got married. But the marriage came to an end four years later because of my continual drinking. Catherine kept our child, Tracey, and although I met up with them briefly twelve years later, I have not seen them since.

After the marriage break-up I returned to my old way of life. In a worse state than ever now, I went to London with my brother and we lived on the streets. I was in and out of prison regularly then – Wandsworth, Brixton, Wormwood Scrubs and finally Northeye semi-open prison in Bexhill. Here I met a visitor to the prison called Susie, who was eventually to become my wife.

Susie takes up the story:

I was the third child of a family of seven, with four brothers and two sisters. My father was a womaniser and seldom at home, but when he was, there were always rows and arguments. The only physical contact between my parents was violent. There was no love whatsoever. My mother would fight for us verbally but I have no memories of any special relationship with either of my parents, ever. My only happy childhood memory is being given a puppy by my dad when I was about two. I can still relive the feelings of joy and excitement that the puppy gave me.

Seven years later my parents' marriage split up, and after Dad left we went onto benefits and there was a big drop in our family income. We could no longer afford to keep the dog, and he had to go. This broke my heart, as I felt he was the only one who loved me, and the feelings of rejection were intense. In the past, when these feelings came, I would curl up with the dog in his basket rather than be parted from him. The first row between my mum and dad that I can remember was over me. I was the only daughter at the time and was always known as "Daddy's little girl". But I had problems with my eyes, which led to my having to wear glasses. Dad couldn't handle this change of image and his attitude towards me changed. I was now "clumsy" and "stupid", and could not do anything right. Somehow I always seemed to need approval from my father but now I never got it.

As a youngster I would wait in the drive at night until bedtime to catch a glimpse of him coming down the road. Invariably he was out late with another woman and I was disappointed. But that did not stop me from doing the same thing the next day – always hoping this would be the time when I could earn his approval and acceptance. I used to hope he would take me to Brownies because I was frightened to go on my own. But even on the odd nights he was home in time he would push me away from him, saying he had not got time for me. A neighbour overheard him once and spoke to him about it, but nothing changed.

So I tried being naughty. When I was seven I stole money from my mother, thinking I would be disciplined with the slipper by my father. I did not care. I actually hoped for this, so desperate was I for some attention. But their means of controlling me was always the threat of taking away the dog that I loved.

I was nine when their marriage broke up. One day my dad was there and the next he wasn't. Our better-than-average lifestyle came to an end. The house and furniture were repossessed and my mother and her five children were put into a halfway house run by Social Services. We had to move to a different area and I joined a new local school. I used to walk home by myself because my mother would wait for my brothers, who came out earlier, but not for me. My route home took me over a manually operated level crossing, and the signalman befriended me and talked to me like a father. He had daughters of his own, and because he was saying the kind of things I had hoped to hear from my own father, I trusted him. Soon I was invited into the signal box and it wasn't long before I was sitting on his lap, unaware of where this was going to lead.

At this time I was made to feel very special. So, of course, I kept going back. It never actually came out into the open, and only stopped when my brother started walking home from school with me. By now my mother was out drinking a lot, and she met a man, who moved into our home. "A real dad!" I thought. "Will he be a real dad to me?" He wasn't. After a while I got invited into bed with him and my mother, and what began innocently enough started developing into something more. Initially, I thought this was what I wanted. I had never experienced any close contact with my real father and I was very open to this new man's careful advances. But he ran as soon as my mother became pregnant, leaving me feeling let down and rejected once again.

The next thing that happened was that my real father reappeared and took me to live with his girlfriend and her two daughters. I hoped that maybe he wanted me there because he missed me. But I was wrong again: I now had to call his girlfriend "Mother", take care of her two children, and help with the housework. During the two years I was there I did not see my real mother once. My stepmother treated me cruelly, wearing me down from a happy-go-lucky girl who chatted easily with anyone to a girl who stuttered badly and finally stopped speaking altogether. This was the last straw for the stepmother. After two years of hell, broken and beaten, I was dumped back on my mother.

My feet had been forced into shoes belonging to my stepsisters – shoes that were much too small for me. I needed four operations to get my feet right. I was now thirteen years old. I had been dropped off at my own mother's in the same clothes I left in two years before. My stepmother's parting words to me were: "In rubbish you arrived, and in rubbish you return." Just what a girl of thirteen needs to make her feel great!

What was becoming clear to me was that the problem they all had with me was simply that I existed at all. I looked forward to being back home, but nothing had changed. My brother who was six years older than me was now "head of the house" and had to be obeyed. Things quickly went wrong. Games of hide-and-seek led to him making me hide with him in the cupboard under the stairs. I repelled his advances because, instead of him saying the tender things I needed to hear, his line was more about me not telling anyone if I wanted to stay out of trouble. The abuse only stopped when he started courting his own girlfriend.

Tossed aside again – that's how I felt! My personality changed. From being abused, I became the abuser. I began bullying anyone who even looked at me – especially my brothers and sisters. I started to miss even the bad experiences I had had, so I began to experiment with my younger brothers, leading them on as I had been led. Then I started to have boyfriends of my own. I knew now what they wanted. And I had no sense of self-worth anyway.

But despite all the abuse I had suffered, I was still techni-
cally a virgin. This was about to change. I did a lot of babysit-
ting for a couple and the husband started to pay me attention.
One night he got me drunk and that was when it all changed,
but that didn't last long, as he soon met other women and I
met other men. For two years I was anybody's, because I was
still desperately searching for love and affection. Sex had no
meaning for me and was merely a passport to a good time. I
was now 18 and the husband I babysat for was in prison for
burglary and alcohol-related offences. I went with his wife to
visit him and found that he shared a cell with someone called
Richie at Northeye, in Bexhill. Under these strange circumstances Richie and I got to know each other! He actually began
to care for me as a person and I knew that at last I had found
someone to whom I was important. He was my world and I
was besotted; there was nothing I wouldn't have done for him!

Richie continues:

When I came out of prison this time, I vowed that things
would change. Susie and I moved into a bedsit and it wasn't
long before Susie became pregnant. But soon after this I was
arrested for burglary and got a one-year sentence. So Susie
had our first child while I was inside, and we named him
Richie, after his dad. When I came out of prison that time, I
decided to join Alcoholics Anonymous, so desperate was I to
get my life straightened out, but the programme did nothing
for me, and I ended up substituting drugs for drink. Starting
with cough mixtures I progressed to cannabis, then speed,
then to injecting any opiates, and finally to heroin. I ended up
dealing cannabis.

When I was arrested again for burglary, I was sentenced
to two-and-a-half years and, as soon as I was released, Susie
fell pregnant again. It was during my next spell in prison that
a prison volunteer working with the probation service visited

me and talked about the Lord. We corresponded for about six months, and I realised that, as a Catholic, I had always believed in Jesus. But although I knew the theology, I had never understood that faith was all about having a personal relationship with Him. I now started to read my Bible seriously, and went to the Church of England prison church instead of chapel. It was on a home leave that Susie and I, now realising the significance of the marriage ceremony, decided to get married.

For a while, everything seemed to be improving for us both. But after about two years I slid back into drugs big time. During this period we had two daughters. I was out of prison for another five years but unfortunately they were five years of hell for the whole family because of my habit. Then I was arrested again, and got sent to Downview Prison Rehabilitation Course. After release I tried Alcoholics Anonymous again, and then Narcotics Anonymous – all to no avail. I felt I was letting God down yet somehow I couldn't make the break. I was on a permanent guilt trip – lots of condemnation, no hope – and eventually depression set in.

I now decided to try an Alpha Course, but this did nothing for me because I felt I knew it all already. Someone suggested that I read *The Bondage Breaker* by Neil Anderson, but still I couldn't find the breakthrough I needed. At this time my local church was running a Freedom in Christ course called "Freedom from Addiction" and I went along to give it a try. We were given a workbook to help us with the course, and we had to keep to a weekly deadline. The discipline of this was a new and challenging experience. Although Susie and I did the course together, we did our workbooks separately. And this brought us together afterwards with a common interest in how we had got on. When we came to the part of the book where Mike and Julia Quarles share their testimony, telling how Mike struggled, as I had, with his addiction, I was able to relate to his experience. And because he had been set free it gave me hope that I might get there too. By working through the book in detail, I was finally brought to the point at which I was able to believe what I already knew, and then I was free. I already knew that Jesus died for me, and in so doing He had won my freedom. And what I found was that as soon as I believed it, I was actually free!

From Susie's angle:

You need to know that, by now, the barriers were up, the frown was in place, the sleeves were rolled up, and I was ready for anyone who tried to upset me. Life had not been easy, and there had come a hardness and a defensive withdrawal from life. My psoriasis flared, stress was very high, and I had constant pain in my stomach – which was diagnosed as irritable bowel syndrome. My neck and shoulders were constantly painful; sometimes I had enough money to feed the family – but when I didn't I had to beg, borrow or steal to put a meal on the table. I still had no sense of self-worth and could not grasp who God really was or what I was to Him.

Just after Richie made his commitment I too became a Christian. But it was only much later that I came to understand what true freedom was. When I read Neil Anderson's *The Bondage Breaker*, I really struggled to believe that I had acceptance, security and significance, because I felt that I had been denied these things for the whole of my life, and I just could not believe that they were mine by right, as a child of God. When I went on the Freedom from Addiction course to get help with my cannabis habit, everything began to fall into place. I could not say at what point things actually changed, but it was as if a light had suddenly been switched on. I believed God loved me as His daughter, regardless of what I looked like or had done, and that as a father He had actually chosen to adopt me unconditionally into His family. At last I'd found my dad!

The testimony of the Quarles made me want to go through the addiction workbook too. I kicked against it at first, but it was the discipline and the Scriptures that helped me through to freedom – "no longer to be subject to a yoke of slavery"! I learned not to rely on how I feel myself, but to rely on Jesus; releasing control to Him was a new experience and allowed me to remain peaceful in times of crisis.

Since doing the course, God has given me a heart for hurting people. I have become a prayer partner in Steps to Freedom appointments, even sometimes bringing a word of knowledge from the Lord. I'm no longer looking over the next hill for the light, because, by God's grace I've found it. Now I want to share it with others.

Richie and Susie sum up:

We are now more together than we have ever been. When Richie was not in prison, although we lived in the same house, we were never actually together. Richie would be upstairs on heroin having his buzz, while Susie would be downstairs having her buzz on cannabis, and seeing to the kids. When it came to bedtime Richie would come downstairs to continue with heroin, while Susie took the kids upstairs to put them to bed and then to continue with her cannabis. Because of the difference in the drugs – cannabis very relaxing and spaced out, heroin more a feeling of well-being and sexual stimulation – the two do not mix in the same room. So we ended up living apart in the same house, separately pursuing our habits. Susie always had to be the one who coped while Richie was away. His return and his freedom caused him to assert himself at home. Susie had trouble coping with that, because her trust had been betrayed so often in the past. Was it real? Would it last? Richie no longer has an excuse to do nothing and since doing the course feels able to handle failure if things go wrong. Before, he would not correct the kids or make decisions for fear of being wrong. Since that change he has been able to take control of his own life and provide effective guidance for those with whom he shares it.

Susie has found that her home, her church and her privacy have all been affected, and in some ways that is difficult to cope with. It has been a time of change and learning – an enjoyable, if at times testing, period in our lives.

Richie has developed a special concern for the homeless particularly, but also for anyone who needs help. He does voluntary work with the homeless at Open House and has completed a computer course via a Job Centre "New Deal". After the work experience he will be in a position to take paid employment if that is God's leading for him. Susie remains a member of the church music group, has some counselling experience, and is involved with children's work inside and outside the church, including an active role on the Youth Development Committee, targeting children with drink and drugs problems. Since coming into freedom Susie has reopened her relationship with her dad and there has been forgiveness and acceptance. Richie has been free of drink and drug addiction for over two years. He experienced no withdrawal symptoms – in itself a miracle. One day he was addicted, and the next day not! He now goes looking for other needy folk through the clubs and pubs in town.

Praise God, we are actually sharing our lives with each other in a way we have never known before!

Like Dissociative Identity Disorder, addiction is often simply a coping mechanism, a way of temporarily switching off the pain of the past. Breakthrough comes when the underlying reasons for the addiction are resolved.

As the hurting person realises the wonderful truth of who they are in Christ and closes the door to any influences of the enemy, they can look their past in the eye. They still won't like what they see there but it will no longer have the hold over them that it did because they know that they are now pure, holy, forgiven children of God.

If you ignore its negative effects on health, relationships and one's ability to stay in touch with reality (and that's a very big "if"!), addiction is an effective coping mechanism. It does blot out the pain for a period and replaces it with a sense of well-being. That makes it a particularly stubborn stronghold and ex-addicts have to do a lot of work on renewing their minds.

Although Richie experienced no physical withdrawal symptoms, you can be sure that, when he is in a tight spot, the old thought patterns will come into play and tell him to have a drink or a joint. A constant commitment to renewing one's mind to the truth in God's word is crucial here.

It's also worth noting that, if a recovering addict has a bad day and goes back to their old coping mechanism, absolutely nothing has changed in the grand scheme of things. Despite the condemnation that the enemy will heap onto them, they are still God's child. God still loves them. The covenant is still in place. They can simply repent of their sin and choose to start again. In no sense have they "blown it" – they've just had a slip up.

In my experience, the support of loving friends is invaluable as addicts go through the process of renewing their minds and the addiction stronghold gradually fades away. It takes time but the good news is that it really is possible in Christ.

Suggestions for further reading

The course Richie went through:

- *Freedom from Addiction* (Anderson & Quarles, Regal, 1996)
- *Freedom from Addiction Workbook* (Anderson & Quarles, Regal, 1997)

A shorter, more easily digestible version of the same teaching:

- *Overcoming Addictive Behaviors* (Anderson & Quarles, Regal, 2003)

Available from your local Christian bookshop or directly from Freedom in Christ Ministries.

Chapter 9

Freedom in ministry

Sometimes people get the impression that tools such as The Steps To Freedom are just for those with "problems". In fact that's not the case at all. I have noticed that churches where the Freedom in Christ approach really takes off are those where the main leaders have submitted themselves to the process first.

Keith is one of the pastors at Goldhill Baptist Church in Buckinghamshire. Here he tells how it's possible to be leader of a church and do lots of "good things" in ministry, yet still not be walking in freedom.

Keith's story

**"My wife, Lynne, wrote on my diary one day.
Its message was loud and clear:
'I want an appointment!'"**

Way back in the early 1980s, while I was working as part of the leadership team of Luton Central Baptist Church, something happened which proved to be a powerful catalyst for change in my own life. As a church we were engaged in a major project. The three town-centre Baptist churches were to be replaced by one main church, creating a single new focus for worship and witness within the town. The plan was to build the new centre on the site of one of the older churches – a site that dated back to 1670.

Soon after the bulldozers moved onto the Park Street site, we were all greeted with some staggering news: the diggers had come to a "dead" stop, literally! As they began the foundations they unearthed a number of deep graves that nobody knew were there – lead-lined tombs dating from the seventeenth century. Immediately the work had to come to a halt, an exhumation order had to be secured, and all those bodies had to be given a more appropriate resting place.

While this was happening, the thought came to me: "You cannot build on dead men's bones." Although the personal significance of this did not hit me at first, a number of events and experiences began to come together and when this happened the impact on me was deeply significant. To explain this fully I need to share something of my earlier years.

I was born in 1950 into a family where life was always very full, often great fun, but usually very hard. I was number five of six surviving children – the sixth, Melvyn, was to be born six years later. Mum and Dad worked very hard not just to put food on the table and clothe us all, but also because they had plans to move off the council estate where we lived in Torquay, and buy their own place. Their dream was to own their own guest house on the "English Riviera", and this they achieved in 1959. The six-bedroomed house cost just £2,000 – an absolute fortune in those days! Guests were due to arrive two weeks after we moved in and we still had gas lighting...

As well as being a science teacher, Dad dug sewers and was an engineer with the Devon General Bus Company and a cultivator of chickens and mushrooms. Mum took in washing, worked part-time in a hotel, and was generally the "hub" of the family. All my brothers and sisters were energetic, hardworking high achievers. I have always been deeply proud of them, and we are now probably closer than we have ever been. In those early years they were often told to look after me, and this meant shutting me in the linen cupboard when I was being a pest! But most of the time I needed their coaching in human survival and I really envied their socially streetwise skills and abilities. I longed for the time when I would know as much as Bryon, could draw like Ray or could make things like Rosemary or Kathleen. Melvyn was to come along later, and he was to become a skilled craftsman with wood. To me, they were all so gifted, and I longed to be like them.

When I left the local secondary-modern school at the age of 16 it was with one "O" level, in Art, a qualification that surely meant that a career in art beckoned! However, my first year at art college was not a deeply pleasant experience. I had excelled at school, but was very average at college. I couldn't understand why I had to learn about art history, or smother a huge canvas with pigment, then ride over it with a bicycle! I simply wanted to be a fine artist!

Looking back, it really was something of a relief when my foundation course was interrupted by a serious motor accident. This was what I consider to be the first of many of God's wake-up calls to me. My weeks of "suspension" in the fracture ward of Torbay Hospital were a salutary awakening to my own frailty. My sister Kathleen had been profoundly influenced by the Salvation Army when she was fourteen and I remember how this affected me personally. Now, in my hour of need, it seemed quite instinctive for me to reach for the Gideon Bible on the bedside table.

It was another three years before I actually did anything about such a trumpet blast from God. The agent for His next nudge forward was a lovely "old lady" – as I thought of her – called Phyl. Phyl was actually still in her fifties. When I left hospital, Dad taught me to drive and I set up my own business selling paraffin from door to door. Phyl was one of my customers. She was different from anyone I had ever met – a born-again Christian, who attended the Baptist "cathedral" in the centre of town. She took the opportunity to witness to me about her faith in God every time I called, and – so I learned later – prayed for me every day for three years.

Phyl was a wonderful example of how to befriend a tradesman. Instead of leaving her money under the paraffin cans as other people did, she would wait for me to knock, then, after serving a welcome plate of beans on toast complete with ashtray, she would talk to me about the importance of knowing Jesus. Even when she didn't need the oil, she would buy it. I found out later that she had a 40-gallon drum in her shed and she kept topping it up!

Eventually, realising that she was "full" and I was running on "empty", I simply said: "Jesus, if all this is true, and you loved me enough to die for me on the cross, then I invite you to come into my life right now." And He did. This was a life-changing experience and the beginning of a relationship with God that turned me "right side up". My mum noticed that something had happened the moment I got in that night, and in a very fumbling and embarrassed way I told her what had happened. Both my parents hoped that it would result in a change for the better. I had not realised how concerned they had been about my lifestyle, which for so long had been totally selfish and reckless.

The stimulation and teaching I received while at Upton Vale was terrific; the fellowship was great too. And it was here that I met a beautiful girl who, within the next two-and-a-half years, would become my wife. From the age of twelve I had played the guitar and very soon after I began to attend Upton Vale I was taken to the "spot coffee-bar", a disused restaurant they were using to evangelise the "mods and rockers" of the day. Usually the place was heaving with teenagers. On this particular night a certain Lynne Mary Vigurs was singing to the accompaniment of a guitarist, and immediately I thought: "I could to that!" Probably the second most profound prayer of my young Christian life was: "Lord, if you can fix it for me to accompany that girl, I will do anything for you!" Within two weeks we were a musical item, and after four weeks I knew we would be married!

Very soon afterwards I sensed God calling me to serve Him full-time, and after three years of studying at the Bible Training Institute in Glasgow (where I achieved the College Diploma, with five "O" levels and two "A" levels), I began a further period of three years training for the Baptist ministry at Spurgeon's College in South Norwood, London. My reason for sharing this personal history is that, even though I had been "soundly converted" and had studied theology, church history, sociology and psychology, there was a gnawing sense of dissatisfaction deep within my life. By 1981 I had been involved in healing and deliverance ministry for a number of years, and had three beautiful children. But it was my experience at Luton during the excavation for the new church building that proved to be both the personal "excavation" and the stirring to a deeper wholeness that I desperately needed.

The fact is that during my years at Luton Central, more than at any other time, I became aware that my life was almost exclusively "performance-orientated" and that this was probably deeply ingrained in my life from my earliest years. The graffiti in my mind shouted continuously: if I did well and worked hard, God would be pleased with me and bless my life and ministry, and even the people I served would love me – it became a vicious circle. I didn't really notice just how totally absorbed I was becoming with my work. I was counselling people, preaching, teaching, organising, administrating, pastoring, evangelising, socialising... and drowning in a sea of busyness and conformity. The reality, I fear, was not conformity to God's expectations but to my own perceptions of what I needed to be and do in order to be accepted and valued.

There came a day when my wife, Lynne, wrote a note in my diary. Its message was loud and clear: "I want an appointment!" I began to suffer from really severe headaches, which were soon impossible to ignore. And the terrible thing was that nobody knew. I was attending charismatic fraternals, conferences and prayer sessions; yet all the time I was feeling a complete failure inside, and nobody knew. It was a very lonely time. Then two important things happened.

The first was that I bit the bullet and went to see my GP. A sensitively perceptive man, he said something like this: "When are you going to realise that you cannot go through life being a man-pleaser? If you carry on like this, you are going to kill yourself. Then what good will you be to God?" At about this time I came across a series of twelve studies by Neil Anderson. The focus of this teaching material was not on what I had to do, but on what God had already done for me: not on who I had to be but who I already was in Christ. All this came to me like a breath of fresh air.

Just as the bulldozers had located those lead-lined vaults, tombs that needed to be excavated so that solid foundations could be built to support the beautiful new church building on Park Street, so I was discovering things about my own hidden life that needed to be challenged and changed – things which had to be brought into line with biblical truths and dynamic spiritual principles. My life and ministry was about to take on a new shape and find a new motivation. Perhaps the words "You cannot build on dead men's bones" should be written on the flyleaf of every Bible – and on every church in the country!

Of course, excavations need time and commitment. I was due to have my first sabbatical leave at this time, and after much thought I decided to spend three months at Regent's Park College in Oxford. It was Trinity term, 1986. I loved it – the beautiful blossom on every quad, the dreaming spires, the rarefied air of centuries of learning, to say nothing of the stimulation of rubbing shoulders with professors, ministers and doctors from all over the world, who gathered in the

Senior Common Room after the lavish lunches... I decided that, as well as my set reading, I would also study the Neil Anderson books systematically, as though I had never read such things ever before. This was not easy, because I had become used to skimming a book to locate facts and illustrations, etc. things that could later be regurgitated to bless others. The trouble was that during this process my own soul's need had so often been bypassed, with what I now saw to be the results.

During this whole three-month period God actually got my attention, and began His excavation into my inner world. As any engineer knows, there are fairly clearly defined steps and ground rules for such a process when preparing land for construction. And when these are followed through, the resulting structure will be stable as well as pleasing to the eye. So I learned that the healing of our inner life is not a haphazard thing, or simply the product of a quick prayer, but a disciplined and systematic application of things God has already revealed in His word. I began to read Neil Anderson's twelve studies and it was as though they were as suited to my need as a glove is to a hand. There was nothing earth-shattering about the material, but instead of being daunted by the sheer scale of the task, and by the haunting thought: "Where do I begin?" I found myself carried naturally along by the logic of it all. The process included The Steps to Freedom in Christ and each Step proved to be deeply significant and manageable, helping me to progress from being a "driven" and performance-orientated person, dominated by activity and the need to be accepted, to a more God-orientated individual enjoying His grace and presence, and knowing His call to service while basking in His approval of me as a son.

But, of course, it is not The Steps themselves that bring freedom. It is Christ. It is knowing and applying His truth that sets us free. Such well-worn steps have proved to be an excellent tool in my experience of true freedom in Christ. I left

Luton Central – a lovely new building, built on a solid foundation – in 1987. Remarkably, God then led me to return to my birthplace, Torquay, to minister on the very estate in Hele where I was born and brought up. This was also deeply significant, as it forced me to grapple with experiences and events from my past that had been conveniently covered up and forgotten.

Having had a new experience of freedom I was hungry for more, and began to dare to "be myself". At first I sought to model it – most important for a leader, I thought – but then I slowly began to teach the little church in Hele village these principles. Over the first six months of my ten years there, I alternated the teaching between morning and evening services and the results were very noticeable. Rather than ministry, which was dislocated from the real needs of people, the material provided substance and a purposeful continuity to my preaching and teaching. Also, during our local ministry of healing, we found that many of the people we prayed with were chronically damaged; yet there were so few places for them to go for help.

I found too that what was so helpful about the Freedom in Christ material was its focus on discipleship rather than on the demonic. It was really helpful for such people to take responsibility for their own lives by working through a structured process towards freedom. Moreover, frequently we saw that prayer ministry or counselling can foster a sense of dependency on the counsellor or "expert", but the Steps to Freedom, in my experience, has the effect of nurturing a greater personal trust in the word of God, as well as individual responsibility and maturity.

In 1997 I joined the staff of Gold Hill Baptist Church. In my present role of directing the pastoral care, I am finding again and again that there are people, like me, who may have been Christians for many years and yet are still emotionally and spiritually crippled by their past experiences and self-defeating behaviour. I am now regularly giving such people the little booklet "The Steps to Freedom in Christ" and helping them to work systematically through the material, till they are liberated into their true inheritance as children of God. The people who have truly understood and applied this biblical teaching are the best equipped to teach others too.

In my experience, Freedom in Christ material is not only helpful for bringing spiritual release for the individual, but can also be used with the whole church. This is particularly important if the fellowship has experienced splits or gross immorality in the past. There is tremendous benefit for a united leadership team systematically working though the material, exploring their past, and dealing with unhelpful roadblocks that prevent them from moving on with God.

It would be wrong for me to imply that since discovering Neil Anderson's books everything has been fine and dandy in my life, or that they have been the only source of blessing to me over the years. God has used many tools, courses and books, written and inspired by inspiring people, to mould, correct and direct my life. I think the thrilling thing about the Freedom in Christ approach has been its simplicity – and the fact that it works. Whenever I have found myself returning to the old "safe" yet enslaving pathways, or listening to the ideas that reinforce the old captivity, I put myself through a refresher course with The Steps and find myself moving forward once again to be the person Christ has called me to be. Not free to do as I like or to be the person I think will please others, but free to be the person God created and called me to be.

That is true liberty!!!

Like Keith, I too find it useful to take myself through The Steps to Freedom on a regular basis, as a kind of spiritual check-up. In fact in the last six months I've done it twice!

One of my favourite aspects of the Freedom in Christ approach is that it works for everyone, from main church leaders through to the newest or most deeply wounded Christian. All Christians face the same basic issues: choosing to repent, believing the truth and winning the battle for our minds. We're all up against the same enemies – the world, the flesh and the devil. All of us are completely dependent on Christ.

In fact, in introducing the approach to a church, it's essential that leaders lead from the front. One leader who has used it to great effect in his church, when asked whether he had had his own Steps to Freedom appointment, said, "I used to be in the army. I would never ask my men to do something I hadn't done myself!"

Another leader told me how powerful it was when she was able to say to a lady with a very traumatic past, who was struggling with the battle for her mind, "Actually, you know, I too get all sorts of thoughts in my mind that aren't true. You need to do what I do, compare them to God's word and make a choice to throw them out if they're not true." The same approach that the leader uses for her own problem areas works for the most deeply wounded person in her church.

We are all in the same boat. No one need be labelled a "hard case" or a "problem person". Yes, some of us have more obviously challenging concerns because of our past experiences. But all of us need to take hold of our freedom in Christ and go on renewing our minds to the truth in God's word. What's more, all of us can! There is no Christian whose past experiences or present circumstances can stop them becoming everything that God wants them to be.

The last story we are going to look at illustrates just how fast Christians can grow if they are taught how to repent and dump any "rubbish" in their lives right at the outset of their Christian life. I have known Pads and Kirstie for a little over three years, ever since Kirstie became a Christian. In that short time I have watched with interest as they have developed an increasingly fruitful ministry in a local church, where they run one of the largest Alpha courses in the area and have seen many people come to know the Lord.

Pads and Kirstie's story

"South Africa and the beach every day was a good tonic for someone whose idea of fun was taking drugs with a crowd of like-minded folk."

Kirstie writes:

I had a happy childhood despite the fact that my parents separated when I was three. Mum did a great job bringing up two girls on her own. She married my stepfather when I was eleven. My stepfather loved me too, despite my resistance! My poor younger sister got the short straw because I bullied her relentlessly. Maybe that is one of the reasons she ended up training to be a counsellor!

We used to go to church every Sunday, which I recall as being very boring and irrelevant. But it was something that was expected of us even when we were at boarding school. Boarding, however, was everything I had hoped it would be – lots of rules to break and plenty of fun to be had. I don't think we ever did anything really serious, though looking back I'm not sure my mother would agree!

I was confirmed at fourteen and remember my mother asking me if I believed in Jesus. This rather took me by surprise, as she never spoke about her faith. My initial response to her question was: "Why – does it really matter?" This seemed to alarm her, so I quickly amended my answer to: "Well, yes..." I wanted to set her mind at rest. Perhaps it really did matter, but I couldn't see why.

By the time I left boarding school I considered myself very

independent, and moved to London with the intention of enjoying life while doing a cookery course. I couldn't even boil an egg at the time!

I had started smoking dope when I was fifteen and that became more regular in London. One thing led to another and I ended up taking all sorts of drugs, discovering that some experiences were more enjoyable than others. Before I knew it, my boyfriend and I were taking heroin every night and things were getting out of hand. But I managed to tell myself, "Use the drugs; don't let the drugs use you..." Incredibly, I never became physically addicted, but my boyfriend was not so lucky. He became really ill and when the family found out what was happening we decided that the best thing to do was to move to Australia.

For a while things seemed better, but it wasn't long before we were back on heroin. Time to head home, we decided, and try to sort things out there. Once we were back in London, however, we split up, and from then on the drugs became less of a daily habit for me. It was at this point that I met Pads, who while certainly enjoying life drew the line at heroin. So we started going to the pub instead. Pads was actually on his way to a job in South Africa when we met, so I ended up joining him there. South Africa and the beach every day was a good tonic for someone whose idea of fun had been taking drugs with a crowd of like-minded people!

A year later, after quite a few drinks one evening, we started reminiscing about friends back home. The outcome was that we decided to get married in England – and in a church! So we set our plans in motion and went for it. The vicar we asked to marry us was an old family friend. He told us that, as we had chosen to marry in God's house, He would be there whether we wanted Him or not! Needless to say we had a great wedding and a wonderful time visiting family and friends for a month before returning to South Africa.

Our son, Tristan, was born two years later and at the same time Pads' company pulled out of South Africa. Returning to England, we settled near Windsor. Our daughter, Kylie, arrived shortly afterwards and we were soon too busy to miss South Africa. We had both the children christened, which I thought of as an insurance policy in case God was real. We started going to our local church once a month because they had a lively family service that was different in a way that made me feel good.

We decided to move further west so that we could have a bigger house and garden in a more rural setting. Our new home was near Reading, and once we were settled in we went to the local church, where all the children were expected to attend Sunday school. Once again, I found the services boring and irrelevant, so we stopped going.

It was some years later that Mum was diagnosed with cancer and died within three months. She planned her own funeral and put everything in order before she died. The church was so packed that we had to have a video link to the marquee. We all missed her terribly. I kept myself busy with anything and everything as I could not really face the pain. My stepfather took the same approach, and kept going on holiday to visit friends until his unexpected death 16 months later.

Pads went to South Africa several months after my mother died and it was at this point that amazing things started to happen. A great friend of his called Chris invited Pads to go with him to his church. Chris had recently become a Christian and had no doubt been praying for Pads, because during the service Pads had an overwhelming sense of the love of God, which was to change his whole life. He came back to England determined to find God in Reading. I found the change in my husband hard to come to terms with and was soon feeling increasingly threatened by it.

We both started an Alpha course in September 2000, as

advised by our friend Chris. Pads finished the course but I dropped out after the first night. But one night Pads came home and told me he had given his life to Jesus. I just could not understand what he meant, and protested that the only person he had given his life to was me – when we got married!

Life became quite difficult after that, especially when Pads announced that he wanted to be baptised. I tried to tell him how I felt, using all the emotional blackmail I could muster in my attempt to knock his new-found faith. I wanted to ensure that I was number one in his life once again. But, despite all my efforts, Pads did not wobble. He just suggested I went on an Alpha course so that I could discover the truth for myself, as I seemed to him to have some strange ideas as to what Christianity was all about.

So I started Alpha again and managed the first few evenings before running away again. Pads hid his disappointment well and decided to take us all to South Africa – back to the very church where he had first experienced the touch of God on his life. We had an amazing holiday, but the earth did not move for me as Pads had hoped it would.

However, on my return to England, I found an invitation to a "Y" course. The purpose of this was to "explore the meaning of life" and it was run by a group of local women. The only thing about the course that appealed to me was that it was run in the mornings – and I normally worked mornings! This seemed like a good excuse to give myself a sabbatical. Pads thought it was a good idea too. So I left my company of seven years and began to attend the "Y" course. I intended to amuse myself with this new venture.

The "Y" course turned out to be a real eye-opener and I realised that I had reached a point where I really did believe Jesus' claims. So it was that on 17 October 2001 I asked Jesus into my life. I remember the day well, as the course leader had asked me to lunch and after lunch she offered me coffee and a prayer. As I didn't have time for both, I chose the prayer!

Afterwards, I phoned Pads and told him what I had done. And it was at that moment that God just filled me with His amazing love. There was no stopping me now. Everyone I spoke to was told about my life-transforming experience and I witnessed passionately for many weeks. Even if people made it plain they were not interested I told them just the same. I was determined to convince them! I can only describe this time as a period when I fell in love with Jesus. "I never knew!" I kept saying to people. "Why did no one tell me about Jesus before?"

I stopped smoking straight away. After 25 years, the desire for cigarettes had just been taken away. Just before my conversion, Pads had started reading Neil Anderson's book *Victory over the Darkness*, and he recommended it to me after I had made my step of faith. I found this book really helpful as I had always had a fear of the dark and of spirits. And I had frightened myself still further by doing Ouija boards at school. Clare, my "Y" course leader, also encouraged me to read the book, as she worked for Neil Anderson's ministry in the UK – Freedom in Christ Ministries. I then read the follow-on book *The Bondage Breaker* and was taken through The Steps to Freedom four weeks later.

I shall never forget arriving at Clare's house for my "freedom appointment" with high expectations but also with a secret store of emotional baggage that I had been doing my best to ignore. I left without the baggage, feeling on top of the world. I soon realised that The Steps are not a quick fix and I needed now to learn how to maintain my new-found freedom. But God had a plan for me and this was that I should help at the Freedom in Christ office for six months. It was here that I was encouraged to take my thoughts captive and renew my mind with God's truth. This has become a way of life for me now, as Jesus intended. And although I am often tempted, and can still be deceived, I feel better equipped to face the world and the enemy.

A little later, Pads had his own freedom appointment, and we were both baptised the following week. Pads had waited to be baptised until I had come to faith, and God had answered his prayers! Our relationship grew much closer and I am happy now to share Pads with God!

In the early summer of 2002 several people, two of whom I had never met before, suggested I do the Introduction to Biblical Counselling Course at Waverley Abbey, run by CWR. I had been interested in counselling for many years and had been doing a secular course while doing the "Y" course, so it seemed an obvious step to take. The teaching was very much in line with Freedom in Christ and it was a great opportunity for me to tune into God afresh as my life was becoming almost too busy to hear what He had to say to me.

It was during that week that God gave me my first mental picture of going into Reading Prison. It was very scary and for nearly a year I kept trying to shut the picture out. Eventually I acknowledged that God was asking me to work for Him in the prison. I needed quite a bit of encouragement but I knew I was in the right place as soon as I started. I helped with a "Y" course in the prison and was always filled with an overwhelming sense of joy every time I went in there.

Pads had been invited to help with the worship in the prison the year before, so he was regularly going to the chapel on a Sunday morning. His early busking days had stood him in good stead! It was shortly after I joined him there that he felt called to full-time ministry, but he was not sure what exactly he was meant to do. He just had a strong sense that it was to begin the following summer. With that in mind, he gave his boss at his computer company nearly a year's notice of his intention and started to see a vocational advisor for the

Church of England. When a position opened up at our church, Pads was asked to join the staff team. This felt right, so we sold our house and downsized for this exciting new step on our journey. Instead of selling computer software, he had become a salesman for God.

I sometimes look back and wonder where we would be without the Freedom in Christ teaching, which helped us to discover, through God's word, our true identity in Christ. I thank God for His amazing grace and all the wonderful opportunities He has given us. We look to Him to help us every day to stand firm in the truth that He has won for us at such great cost.

Pads and Kirstie both came into their Christian life with a fair bit of "baggage". Although they are too modest to include many details in their story, most around them would agree that their growth to maturity and fruitfulness has been astonishingly fast. Both they and I put this down to the fact that they dumped their baggage right at the start of their new-found walk with the Lord by going through The Steps to Freedom.

What excites me more than anything is the prospect of churches around the country helping new Christians do the same.

If we are honest, many in our churches fall into the same category as the Corinthians:

> **Brothers, I could not address you as spiritual but as worldly – mere infants in Christ. I gave you milk, not solid food, for you were not yet ready for it. Indeed, you are still not ready. (1 Corinthians 3:1, 2)**

The literal meaning of the Greek word that has been translated "ready" in this passage is "able". Paul says he could not give the Corinthians the "solid food" of more advanced teaching because they were not "able" to receive it. Maturity is not simply a question of wanting to move on. Many sincere Christians desperately want to, but they are not able to. They need to resolve their personal and spiritual conflicts.

The writer to the Hebrews identified a similar problem:

> **Though by this time you ought to be teachers, you need someone to teach you the elementary truths of God's word all over again. You need milk, not solid food! Anyone who lives on milk, being still an infant, is not acquainted with the teaching about righteousness. But solid food is for the mature, who by constant use have trained themselves to distinguish good from evil. (Hebrews 5:12–14)**

They were not moving on because they had not grasped the basic truths of the Gospel, specifically the teaching about what made them righteous. So many in our churches have the right doctrine but have not really connected with the deep but simple truth that they are now children of God – pure, holy, forgiven and loved; that they are welcome into God's presence at any time with no condemnation.

If every new Christian were given the opportunity to resolve their personal and spiritual conflicts and really got hold of what it means to be a child of God right at the start of their Christian life, I suspect that the church would be a different place.

The wonderful truth is that no Christian needs to go round and round in circles. Every one can go on to maturity and fruitfulness, no matter what is in their past or what their present circumstances are.

The Good News that Jesus came to bring is just as effective today as it's ever been. It can work in your life. It can work in your church.

Chapter 10

Claiming your freedom in Christ

I have personally met many of the people whose stories are told in this book. In some cases I have seen both the "before" and the "after" and it has been a real privilege to watch as they have doggedly taken hold of truth even though, to start with at least, it often didn't feel true at all.

These stories are by no means unique. All around the world Christians are discovering that Jesus' promises of freedom and abundant life apply to them today, no matter how difficult their past or present circumstances. Freedom In Christ Ministries has a particular approach that it shares with churches who want to use it, but I'm always at pains to point out that it's not our approach that sets people free, it's Jesus Christ.

Has reading these stories made you aware of areas in your own life where you are not walking in the freedom that He has won for you? If you feel you need some pointers as you take hold of your own freedom in Christ, this chapter is for you.

First, a couple of important principles.

Nothing is too difficult for Jesus

The good news is that nothing is too hard for Jesus, and no Christian is too "messed up" for Him to heal, and heal completely. You can have every expectation of coming through to complete freedom with the loving support of your church.

It may not feel like it right now, but the Bible makes clear that Jesus has already given you everything you need in order for you to be free, whole and fulfilled (see 2 Peter 1:3, Ephesians 1:3). It's all yours – all the freedom and joy you could ever want or need. He did all the hard work for us in His death and resurrection. You can be assured that you now have all the resources of heaven to draw upon in order to come though to complete wholeness.

If you are not yet a Christian, that's easy to put right! Simply make a choice to acknowledge your need of Jesus, thank Him for dying to forgive your sins and giving you back spiritual life, and tell Him that you choose to give Him control of your life.

There are things that only you can do

Each of us has responsibilities before God. There are some things that only you can do, and some choices that only you can make.

Only you can choose to obey God, to forgive others, to say "yes" to Him and "no" to wrong ways of thinking or behaving. Nobody else can do it for you. Others can help you and provide the best environment possible, but in the end your freedom will boil down to what *you* choose to believe and do.

That may sound like bad news if you have come to believe that you are helpless and need the help of some special person to set you free, or if you are waiting for God to do something. But actually it's very good news because it means that nothing and no one can keep you from becoming the person God wants you to be. You don't need some specially anointed person to do the right thing or say the right words. Neither is there anything more that God needs to do. Everything that needed to happen for you to be free in Christ happened 2,000 years ago at the cross. It's in your hands – and if God Himself wants you to do it, He will give you everything you need along the way.

I know, however, that it may well not feel like that at all right now. In fact, you may well feel trapped and hopeless. That simply means that you have probably come to believe all kinds of lies about yourself and what has happened to you, lies that come from the enemy.

These lies can be so deeply ingrained that they become "strongholds" – places where you have got stuck in old habits and ways of thinking that are harmful for you, and from which you feel (wrongly) unable to escape.

No matter what you feel, the truth is that you are totally accepted and embraced by your heavenly Father. You are definitely not a failure, and you have a really important place in His kingdom. You may feel you don't deserve God's love – that's true; none of us does. But God has offered it to all of us as a gift – and that includes you. He loves you as His child and only wants to lavish good things on you – no matter what you have done or what has been done to you. So, as the opportunity comes to reach out for a new way of living, let me encourage you to "go for it". There is such a good life ahead of you.

So where should you start?

1. Know who you are in Christ

I would suggest that first of all you get hold of the main Freedom In Christ teaching that focuses particularly on your new identity in Christ as well as understanding the spiritual battle you are in and how to win it. There are various ways of doing that. You could:

- read *Victory over the Darkness* and *The Bondage Breaker* by Neil Anderson;
- attend The Freedom in Christ Discipleship Course (known as Beta – The Next Step In Discipleship in the USA and elsewhere) at your church;
- go through the course on your own using the DVD/videos or audio tapes available from Freedom in Christ Ministries;

- attend a Living Free in Christ conference (held regularly around the country).

2. Go through The Steps to Freedom in Christ

The Bible makes clear that we are all in a spiritual battle. We have an enemy who wants to stop us entering into all that Jesus has won for us. The good news, however, is that we have everything we need to deal with him. If we submit to God and resist the devil, he has no choice but to run away from us (James 4:7).

Part of submitting to God involves specifically turning our backs on things that we have done in the past that may have given the enemy what Paul calls a "foothold" in our lives. This is called "repentance". In doing this we specifically close any door that we opened to the enemy in our lives.

The Steps to Freedom in Christ, which everybody whose story is in this book went through, is simply a structured way to do this. You ask the Holy Spirit to show you if there are any areas in your life that need to be dealt with, and when He shows you, you simply choose to renounce them. It's a kind and gentle process that typically takes three to five hours and is best done in the context of your own church with a supportive leader or friend to encourage you and, ideally, someone to pray for you while you are doing it.

You will need a copy of *The Steps to Freedom in Christ* booklet. You may like to use The Steps to Freedom in Christ DVD/video session, which is also available to guide you through the process.

Many are amazed by how clear their mind becomes when they have completed this process. Why? Because the enemy's ability to confuse their thinking has been taken away.

The Steps process is not the end of the story, however. In fact in many ways it's just the beginning.

3. Constantly renew your mind

It is crucial to learn to stand firm in the freedom gained.

Often, through what we were taught when we were very young, or because of things that have happened to us, we have received messages that have been harmful to us or are simply untrue. Our minds easily get "stuck" in these harmful ways of thinking and, even when we become Christians, no one presses a "clear" button.

Perhaps we have learned to believe that we are failures, or not loved, or that nobody wants us. Even when we know on one level that, for example, abuse was not our fault, or that things really can get better, somehow it is hard to shift these gut beliefs. The Steps process may well help us uncover some of the lies we have believed but it doesn't automatically replace them with truth.

If we don't actively take steps to replace these old ways of thinking based on lies with new ways based on truth, we will not go on to walk in the freedom gained.

Once we have become aware of deep-rooted lies we have believed, we need to go through a process the Bible calls "renewing the mind". That is, we have to, bit by bit, kick out the lies that make us feel so lousy and fearful, and take on board the truth of how important and significant we are to God and His kingdom; how loved we are; how protected and strong we are in the face of the enemy. When we are afraid and anxious we become tense and our bodies and minds stop working the way they should. So quite often when we renew our minds we find lots of other things improve and we feel much, much better in every way.

Neil Anderson's book *Walking in Freedom* is very helpful in this, and is specifically written to help you follow up The Steps to Freedom process. I also recommend a strategy I call "stronghold-busting", which was mentioned in some of the stories you have read in this book. This is explained in some detail in Session 10 of the Freedom in Christ Discipleship Course and we covered it in an earlier chapter. Here is a summary:

1. First of all, you need to determine the lie you have been believing (any way you are thinking that is not in line with what God says about you in the Bible). You will become aware of what these are as you go through the Steps process. The key thing is to ignore what you feel but commit yourself wholeheartedly to God's truth.

2. Then, find as many Bible verses as you can that state the truth and write them down. A good concordance (or helpful pastor) will come in useful.

3. Write a prayer or declaration based on the formula:

- I renounce the lie that…
- I announce the truth that…

4. Finally, read the Bible verses and say the prayer/declaration every day for 40 days, all the time reminding yourself that God is truth and that if He has said it, it really is true for you. Remember that, for most of the 40 days, the stronghold-busting exercise will *feel* like a waste of time. Grit your teeth, hang on and persevere to the end!

Here's an example of a completed stronghold-buster I did to help me with a weakness I have for comfort eating.

Taking comfort in food rather than God

The lie: that overeating brings lasting comfort.

Proverbs 25:28
Like a city whose walls are broken down is a man who lacks self-control.

Galatians 5:16
So I say, live by the Spirit, and you will not gratify the desires of the sinful nature.

Galatians 5:22–24
But the fruit of the Spirit is love, joy, peace, patience, kindness, goodness, faithfulness, gentleness and self-control. Against such things there is no law. Those who belong to Christ Jesus have crucified the sinful nature with its passions and desires.

2 Corinthians 1:3–4
Praise be to the God and Father of our Lord Jesus Christ, the Father of compassion and the God of all comfort, who comforts us in all our troubles, so that we can comfort those in any trouble with the comfort we ourselves have received from God.

Psalm 63:4–5
I will praise you as long as I live, and in your name I will lift up my hands. My soul will be satisfied as with the richest of foods; with singing lips my mouth will praise you.

Psalm 119:76
May your unfailing love be my comfort.

Lord, I renounce the lie that overeating brings lasting comfort. I announce the truth that you are the God of all comfort and that your unfailing love is my only legitimate and real comfort. I affirm that I now live by the Spirit and do not have to gratify the desires of the flesh. Whenever I feel in need of comfort, instead of turning to foods I choose to praise you and be satisfied as with the richest of foods. Fill me afresh with your Holy Spirit and live through me as I grow in self-control. Amen.

Tick off the days

1	2	3	4	5	6	7	8	9	10
11	12	13	14	15	16	17	18	19	20
21	22	23	24	25	26	27	28	29	30
31	32	33	34	35	36	37	38	39	40

Getting help to work through the process

Although it is possible to work through the process on your own, I strongly recommend that you do that only if there really is no other option available to you. In one sense you are the one who will do all the work, but it makes all the difference in the world to have the support and encouragement of caring Christians beside you. It has been well said: "You alone can do it, but you can't do it alone."

In our experience there are many Christians out there who are more than happy to help a hurting soul, even if they don't quite know how. If you are not currently in a church, I would encourage you to get involved in one, ideally one that understands the Freedom in Christ approach.

Start by talking to your church leaders. Let them know that, although Freedom in Christ Ministries does not help individuals directly, we are always happy to offer support and guidance to church leaders who are helping people through the process. Christians around you are the very best people to help you long-term, for they are the ones who know and love you. They are on the spot when you need them, and can be far more effective in loving and teaching you on a weekly or even daily basis.

There is great hope for you. God loves to mend broken lives – in fact He mended you when He sent Jesus to die for you. God bless you as you seek the truth that will set you free.

It is my prayer that this book has given you hope both for your own church and for your own life. We really do have abundant life in Christ. Let's live in it!

Chapter 11

Freedom in your church

The church has what the world needs

A woman contacted the Freedom in Christ office and said, "My best friend had clinical depression and went through The Steps to Freedom and has been better ever since. Can you arrange for me to do it too because I suffer from depression as well?" Asked if she was a Christian, she said she was not, and was, therefore, informed that the process would not work for her because it is based on the fact that Christians become completely new creations when they receive Christ. Her response was: "Can you please tell me how to become a Christian?"

Low self-esteem, depression, anxiety, addictions, eating disorders… Aren't these the major problems faced by all modern societies? When the world sees people genuinely resolving these things, won't they sit up and take notice? Won't they want to know what it is that we in the church have that makes such a difference? When they understand that what we have is the free gift of new life in Christ, won't they want it too?

I can envisage local churches holding open meetings during which Christians explain how they found their freedom from depression or addiction and offering to get alongside those who are still suffering. That is surely the reality that people are looking for.

Will the Lord send revival?

Yet what happens when people with these problems become Christians? They are carrying a lot of baggage. There are a lot of things that they need to resolve. That's not particularly difficult now that they are new creations, but if they join a church that is unable to help them close the doors in their lives that are open to the enemy's influence or explain to them how to take hold of their freedom in Christ and stand firm, what is the likely outcome? They will probably make a genuine attempt to do their best at "being a Christian" but will become increasingly troubled by the negative thoughts in their minds or the patterns of sin they don't seem to be able to break, and eventually give up.

A lot of people in our churches are doing their best to "act like Christians" in the hope that they will become "like everyone else". They end up either living a kind of double life or walking away. The irony, of course, is that the answer comes when they realise that they don't have to "act" like a Christian, they simply have to be themselves: pure, holy, new creations who have the power and authority to kick the enemy out of their lives and grow.

I suspect that the Lord wants to send revival to the church. However, we need to think through the consequences of what that means. People are increasingly growing up without any Christian influence in their lives. They are opening more and more doors in their lives to the enemy. When they finally realise the truth and turn to Christ, they are going to need some guidance on resolving the problems those activities have caused and getting rid of the enemy's influence. I suspect that the Lord won't send revival until His church is ready to receive those who will come in.

Making disciples

For too long in the Western church, we have concentrated on making *converts* – simply bringing people into the kingdom – rather than on making *disciples*, people who are growing, maturing and bearing fruit.

Where we have had an expectation of breakthrough in people's lives, it's often been in the context of people "having something done to them", whether it's deliverance ministry, prayer ministry, counselling or being "zapped" by an "anointed" person. There may be value in all those things, especially if they involve the individual repenting and acting on the truth, but we have signally failed to help people understand the key truth: that, in Christ, they already have everything they need to live a godly life (2 Peter 1:3; Ephesians 1:3).

God places the responsibility for resolving personal and spiritual conflicts and moving on to maturity firmly in the hands of the individual. Because He is not a cruel God who demands that people do something that's impossible, we can conclude that every single Christian in your church can become everything that God wants them to be. They themselves are the only people who can get in the way of that being accomplished. We do our people a great disservice if we give them the impression that resolution of their problems is out of their hands and depends on someone else doing something for them.

The Gospel really works!

We are the Body of Christ. We are here in the world to do His work, to carry on His anointing. Jesus told us clearly what that work was when He stood up in the synagogue at Nazareth (Luke 4:16ff.), read from the scroll of Isaiah and said, "Today this scripture is fulfilled in your hearing."

Let's look at Isaiah 61, the passage He read (the comments in square brackets are mine):

> **The Spirit of the Sovereign LORD is on me, because the LORD has anointed me to preach good news to the poor [this Hebrew word literally means "pressed down" or "depressed", in either mind or circumstances]. He has sent me to bind up the**

broken-hearted, to proclaim freedom for the captives and release [this term refers to "opening", as in the opening of eyes to the truth or the opening of a dungeon] from darkness for the prisoners [people who are tied up in bonds], to proclaim the year of the LORD's favour and the day of vengeance of our God, to comfort all who mourn, and provide for those who grieve in Zion – to bestow on them a crown of beauty instead of ashes, the oil of gladness instead of mourning, and a garment of praise instead of a spirit of despair [could also be translated "weakness" or "being in darkness" or "heaviness"].

The good news that Jesus came to bring is specifically for those who are depressed, those who feel like prisoners, those who don't know the truth, those who are mourning and grieving, those who are weak or in darkness.

As the passage continues, we see a glorious truth emerge:

They will be called oaks of righteousness, a planting of the LORD for the display of his splendour. They will rebuild the ancient ruins and restore the places long devastated; they will renew the ruined cities that have been devastated for generations.

Who is it who become those strong oaks of righteousness that will display the splendour of the Lord? Who is it who will do the work of rebuilding, restoring and renewing? It's the very people who were depressed, in bondage, weak and in darkness.

That is the glorious good news! We can expect the very people who seem the most hopeless or downtrodden to be the ones used mightily by God. That is not to say, of course, that He doesn't delight in using all His people, but His splendour and glory are made more obvious when the apparently hopeless are turned around completely. Can you really expect those with serious problems in your church to become genuinely fruitful disciples? Yes, yes and yes again! Isn't that the Gospel?

What's at stake here is not the reputation of a particular ministry or approach but that of the church. What's on God's heart is even bigger than seeing individuals' lives turned around:

> **His intent was that now, through the church, the manifold wisdom of God should be made known to the rulers and authorities in the heavenly realms, according to his eternal purpose which he accomplished in Christ Jesus our Lord. (Ephesians 3:10–11)**

As you help people in your church to find their freedom in Christ and move on to become fruitful disciples, God's multi-faceted wisdom is being demonstrated to the heavenly realms. Those satanic beings who sneer at God, who want the world to believe that the Gospel doesn't work and who accuse His people are put to shame as the wonderful truth shines through for all to see.

Getting started in your church

In no way am I saying that the approach to discipleship from Freedom in Christ Ministries is the only way that your church can see people's lives changed. It is Jesus Christ who makes that possible, not a particular approach to ministry. However, I recommend the Freedom in Christ approach as a good and effective way of making disciples and helping your people move on to maturity. If you want to get your church up and running, here is a suggested way forward:

1. Get the commitment of the leaders

Perhaps the most crucial factor in whether a "freedom ministry" is successful is the commitment of the leadership, and specifically the main leader. I strongly recommend that leaders go through the teaching and have their own individual freedom appointments ahead of everyone else. If your leaders are not yet fully committed, wait patiently until they are.

2. Get key people up to speed

You will want to make sure that other key people are with you: cell or small-group leaders, those responsible for pastoral care, and so on. You could invite them to a Freedom in Christ conference, give them the main books (*Victory over the Darkness* and *The Bondage Breaker*) to read or refer them to the Freedom in Christ website.

3. Get some experience in running Steps to Freedom appointments

In an ideal situation the first people to have their own personal freedom appointments will be leaders. If possible it would be good for a couple of people to have their appointments with others who are experienced (i.e. from outside the church), simply to get an appreciation of how an appointment works. They can then take other people through. It would be good for a key team to attend a Freedom in Christ "Get Started with the Freedom in Christ Approach" event which gives guidelines, hints and tips, but if there is no course available in the near future in your area don't let that stop you getting started; simply take each other through the process. You will learn as you go along that it does not depend on the skill of the encourager but on the fact that Jesus always turns up. Freedom in Christ can usually arrange freedom appointments for leaders (normally up to two from a church) in order that they can then go back and take others through.

4. Introduce the teaching to the church

You are now ready to start teaching at a church-wide level. The best way of doing this is by using The Freedom in Christ Discipleship Course. Do not feel that you have to cover everyone at once – starting small works well and gives leaders the chance to get familiar with the material in a smaller setting. Take it slowly – this is not generally something that a church does for a term but something that becomes part of "business as usual". As such it's well worth while planning it properly to make sure that it does not fizzle out before the positive effects have been felt.

5. Set up a process for running freedom appointments

As you teach the material, gradually introduce the concept of freedom appointments and plan how you are going to administer appointments. As the teaching nears an end, start to offer individual appointments – resist the temptation to start with those who seem in dire need but gain some experience with those who are more likely to be straightforward. Insist that freedom seekers complete the basic teaching before their freedom appointment, so that they know how to stand firm afterwards.

6. Build your team of "encouragers"

Encouragers are those who lead the freedom appointments, so-called because their role is not to be an expert but simply to encourage the freedom seeker to choose to repent, forgive and believe the truth. You will find that those who have been through the teaching and had their own appointment can often become encouragers fairly quickly so that the burden is shared. This is generally a ministry for non-experts and has the benefit of removing much of the pastoral burden from leaders.

7. Emphasise the need to make it a way of life

Although the results are often dramatic, avoid portraying this as a "quick fix". Instead, emphasise that every freedom seeker will need to apply ongoing effort to maintain the freedom gained and continue to grow as a disciple. Put a lot of emphasis on helping people maintain the progress they have made by encouraging them to keep renewing their minds, using "stronghold-busting" or another approach. You might run nurture groups. Encourage people to have freedom appointments on an annual basis, as the spiritual equivalent of having their car serviced regularly.

As you go through the process, keep emphasising that this is discipleship for everyone – not just for "hard cases" – and look out for the enemy's attack, often through the least expected people.

Freedom in Christ Ministries is always ready to offer advice to church leaders and to help in any way it can. A good place to start are our websites: www.ficm.org.uk or www.ficm.org. Neil Anderson has written excellent books that give much deeper treatments of matters such as addiction, depression, fear, sexual problems, self-esteem and so on. Details are available on our website. The key books I would advise church leaders to read in the first instance are *Victory over the Darkness* and *The Bondage Breaker* for the basic teaching and *Discipleship Counselling* to understand the theological basis of The Steps to Freedom in Christ and how to use it practically in your own setting.

Go for it!

I hope that you have been encouraged to see that God uses ordinary people in ordinary churches to accomplish truly extraordinary things, the effect of which reaches even to the heavenly realms themselves.

Is there any reason why you should not see the same things happening – or happening to a greater degree than they are at the moment – in your church? The wonderful thing is that everything that needed to take place for us to see lives transformed in our churches has already happened. It happened when Jesus suffered and died on that cross outside Jerusalem and then burst out of the tomb to new life.

We are the Church of Jesus Christ and the gates of hell cannot prevail against us!

Contacting Freedom in Christ Ministries

In the UK:

If you are an individual looking for help, in the first instance please talk to your church leader and advise them of the support that Freedom In Christ can give them as they support and encourage you.

Church leaders – take a look at www.ficm.org.uk and, if you feel we can encourage or equip you, please get in touch with us at:

Freedom in Christ Ministries
PO Box 2842
Reading RG2 9RT
UK
E-mail: info@ficm.org.uk

In the USA:

Contact:
Freedom in Christ Ministries
9051 Executive Park Drive
Suite 503
Knoxville, TN 37923
USA
Phone: 865-342-4000
Fax: 865-342-4001
www.ficm.org

Other Countries:

Details of other Freedom in Christ Ministries international offices are available at www.ficm.org.

Freedom In Christ In The UK

Freedom In Christ

Church leaders – can we help you make disciples?

Although the Church may have made some *converts*, most will agree that we have made few real *disciples*. Far too many Christians struggle to take hold of basic biblical truth and *live it out*. It's not as if we lack excellent teaching programmes. It's more to do with people's ability to "connect" with truth. Or, as Jesus put it, "You will *know* the truth and the truth will set you free." (John 8:32)

Many churches in the UK now use the Freedom In Christ approach to help Christians make connections with truth and mature into fruitful disciples. It works well as: a church-wide discipleship programme; a follow-up to introductory courses like Alpha; a cell equipping track; or a small group study.

If you are a UK church leader, we are at your disposal. We run a regular programme of conferences and training, and are always happy to offer advice.

Send for our catalogue

Send for our full colour catalogue of books, videos and audiocassettes. It includes resources for churches and for individuals (including children and young people and specialist areas such as depression and addiction).

Join the Freedom Fellowship

For those using the Freedom In Christ approach, the Freedom Fellowship provides advice on getting started in your church and regular news and encouragement.

For details of any of the above, see www.ficm.org.uk, e-mail info@ficm.org.uk or write to us at:
Freedom In Christ Ministries, PO Box 2842, READING RG2 9RT.

www.ficm.org.uk

Freedom In Christ Ministries is a company limited by guarantee (number 3984116) and a registered charity (number 1082555). It works by equipping local churches to help Christians claim their freedom in Christ and become fruitful disciples.